Rescuing the Experience

Innovations in Education

Series Editor : Colin Fletcher (Lecturer in the School of Policy Studies, Cranfield Institute of Technology)

There have been periods of major innovation in public education. What do the achievements amount to and what are the prospects for progress now? There are issues in each slice of the education sector. How have the issues come about?

Each author analyses their own sphere, argues from experience and communicates clearly. Here are books which speak both with and for the teaching profession; books which can be shared with all those involved in the future of education.

Three quotations have helped to shape the series:

> "The whole process – the false starts, frustrations, adaptions, the successive recasting of intentions, the detours and conflicts – needs to be comprehended. Only then can we understand what has been achieved and learn from experience." *Marris and Rein*
>
> "In this time of considerable educational change and challenge the need for teachers to write has never been greater." *Hargreaves*
>
> "A wise innovator should prepare packages of programmes and procedures which . . . could be put into effect quickly in periods of recovery and reorganisation following a disaster." *Hirsh*

Current titles in the series

Bernard Barker : Rescuing the Comprehensive Experience
Jan Stewart : The Making of the Primary School

Rescuing the Comprehensive Experience

Bernard Barker

Open University Press

Milton Keynes · Philadelphia

Open University Press
Open University Educational Enterprises Limited
12 Cofferidge Close
Stony Stratford
Milton Keynes MK11 1BY, England
and
242 Cherry Street
Philadelphia, PA 19106, USA

First Published 1986

British Library Cataloguing in Publication Data
Barker, Bernard
  Rescuing the comprehensive experience. –
(Innovations in education)
  1. Comprehensive high schools – Great Britain
  I. Title   II. Series
  373.2'5'0941   LA635

  ISBN 0–335–15141–8
  ISBN 0–335–15116–7 Pbk

Library of Congress Cataloging in Publication Data
Barker, Bernard.
    Rescuing the comprehensive experience.
    Includes index.
    1. Comprehensive high schools – England.
    2. Educational equalization – England.   I. Title.
LA635.B345 1985   373.2'5'0942   85–11505

ISBN 0–335–15141–8
ISBN 0–335–15116–7 (pbk.)

Typeset by Rowland Phototypesetting Limited
Bury St Edmunds, Suffolk
Printed in Great Britain by St Edmundsbury Press
Bury St Edmunds, Suffolk

for Chris and Irene Barker

Contents

Contents

Contents

ix

Diagrams and examples

Acknowledgements

I owe my colleagues and pupils past and present, especially those at Stanground School, Peterborough, a great debt for their constant stimulus and friendship. I should like to thank more particularly the Master and Fellows of Gonville and Caius College, Cambridge, and Cambridgeshire County Council for jointly funding the schoolteacher fellow commonership that enabled the final draft of this book to be written in comfort and peace; Rex and Eileen Tregunna for support, encouragement and a vision of how success for all may be achieved; Colin Fletcher for his sympathetic editing; and my wife for so long tolerating my passion for school.

Series editor's foreword

Bernard Barker meets his readers in the rooms and corridors of a modern comprehensive school. We see many details through his eyes. We realise the significance of these details when he puts taken-for-granted principles under pressure. He reminds us of classroom feelings, of tests, of playgrounds and of the pieces of broken urgency which make up adolescence. He recalls, especially for teachers, the breakthroughs in drumming up interest for their own subject. He makes discussions on management and curriculum genuinely meaningful.

All this astute observation and careful discussion pursues Bernard Barker's clearly stated aim. He tests here 'the inescapable claim of the comprehensive that all children, of whatever ability or background, should be educated together and will benefit profoundly from the shared experience'.

This series of books, 'Innovations in Education', is guided by three general principles. First, the innovations of the more idealistic and optimistic 1960s and early 1970s are to be carefully assessed. Bernard Barker gets to the heart of debates that have shelves of specialised texts and manuals devoted to them, and those innovations that he judges worthwhile are given their rightful place. The second principle is to draw upon personal experience. Bernard Barker is here amongst the very first of a new breed – an ex-pupil of a comprehensive who became a headteacher at a comprehensive when thirty-four. This book gives more facts about the feelings in schools than any research project has tried to do. Third, all the issues, problems and potentials are addressed with the authority of a practitioner. There is no separate social science framework for different matters to hang upon; nor is there a neat exclusion of intense conflicts. Instead he explores how it is practical 'to open the way for the changes necessary . . . to create a distinctive authentically comprehensive pattern of education and a more democratic society'.

Colin Fletcher

Preface

I was a boy at one of the earliest and largest comprehensive schools in London (Eltham Green, 1957–65) and am Head of another rather like it in Peterborough (Stanground, 1980–). It has been a long and rather lonely education. No one else from my school went up to Cambridge; none of my friends or contemporaries in teaching were at comprehensive schools themselves. With rare exceptions the Heads or Deputies I know were brought up at grammar or public schools. My experiences are sufficiently uncommon to make good fiction, somewhere between Rudyard Kipling and the Marx Brothers. But *Rescuing the Comprehensive Experience* is not a memoir or anecdotal history. It is, rather, an attempt to make sense of ideas derived from my own continuing education and to investigate how the common school can fulfil its original purpose.

My socialist father sent me to Eltham Green to take part in a social experiment. It was the most daring thing he ever did and he hoped that class and privilege would dissolve as children shared a common experience of learning. A new, democratic society without masters or servants would be forged in the Promethean fire of knowledge. It was the vision of an elementary schoolboy rehoused by the London County Council (LCC) on a model estate in Tottenham. His belief in fraternity and community conflicted unconsciously with a desire for my own success and advancement. This unresolved ambivalence, shared by a generation of teachers and parents, has bedevilled comprehensive education.

Eltham Green was a shining glass palace filled with excitement where it did briefly seem that equality was in sight. Once the barriers of social privilege and the eleven-plus were torn down, anything was possible. The comprehensive school offered the means through which an effective mass democracy, free of ignorance and subservience, might emerge. As a boy I longed for equality. As a teacher my ambition and purpose have been to educate for equality, to awaken pupils to their responsibilities as free citizens, to prepare them to decide questions that should not be left to experts or a managerial class. Sometimes this rather Fabian exercise has seemed successful, bringing under one ambitious roof children from the most diverse backgrounds. Over twenty years, good, established comprehensives have developed an informal, reasonably united society within their walls, offering a genuine equality of opportunity in an immense variety of activities. Pupils who might have been tainted for life by the eleven-plus have progressed together through an increasingly common curriculum and experience. More of them take and pass examinations than ever before, and British children are as confident, unsnobbish and skilful as they have ever been. Comprehensives are not easily managed and even those that underestimate their pupils often deserve recognition for fairness and efficiency.

At times I despair at the continuing, unchanging passivity of a great many youngsters whose energies and interests seem untouched by the business of school. If children are to extend their control over their own lives, something quite new is needed. Most of our teaching is conventional and inadequate for the opportunity presented by the common school. There are, of course, reasons for this failure to mobilise the talent and commitment of millions of children that are wholly unconnected with lessons. Youngsters play truant because they cannot cope with their homes, not because the curriculum is deficient. There is a social geography of low achievement as there is of ill-health or voting behaviour.

Yet, from my early days at Eltham Green, I have been uneasy about the methodology and organisation of comprehensives. I was placed in a 'flying' group, taking 'O' levels early. Comradeship or cooperation was incidental to the main principle of the school. The idea was to divide children according to their scores on intelligence tests and to hustle the 'best' through as many examinations as possible. The curriculum was based on specialised subjects derived from an academic tradition; essay writing, competition and individual progress preoccupied parents and teachers. Once the egalitarian images were set on one side, Eltham Green failed the great mass of its pupils by its very preoccupation with success. The classroom experience remained as divisive and as unlikely to lead to enhanced citizenship as that offered in grammar or secondary modern schools. Teachers did not rethink their assumptions or strategies; instead they sought out the same clever boys and girls they had always looked for and found. These were coached to become specialists able to manage and administer their fellows.

Altogether I sat fourteen GCE 'O' level examinations, including repeats, spread over six different seasons between the ages of fourteen and eighteen. I passed eight and failed six. At the time it seemed an almost futile drudgery and I diverted myself by captaining the chess team, editing and typing the school magazine, debating, acting and dashing down the wing for the hockey XI. Such activities brought pupils and teachers together through shared enthusiasms. I learned most of what makes my present job possible from extracurricular pursuits. The Latin, Additional Mathematics and Chemistry contributed rather less to my understanding. The 420 children in forms below mine on admission day 1957 found even less pleasure in lessons, and did not prolong school for the sake of games.

Citizenship was not included in the curriculum for the majority of pupils, who were prepared for working lives as typists, clerks and woodworkers, the latter occupation already almost vanished. Feeble though they were, my examination results ensured my separation from the neighbourhood and community of which the school was supposed to be the focus and in which my father believed. Children left to pursue diverse careers and did not see one another again. The experience of education emptied rather than strengthened neighbourhoods.

The teaching arrangements adopted in most comprehensives tend to reinforce the difficulties that impede all but a small number of highly literate pupils from achieving recognisable success or enjoying learning. Active, educated citizenship is as remote as ever, and the 'excellence' of the few is prized above the possibilities of the many. This implicit contradiction between the social symbolism and potential of the common school and current educational manoeuvres provides a compelling motive for re-examining and reforming the theory and practice of learning.

The 'comprehensive experience' has to be rescued from its own meritocratic assumptions about children and teaching before it can be saved from politicians, falling rolls or shrinking finances. A distinctive comprehensive learning programme must be devised to establish the common school as the hub of an educated and democratic community. This rescue bid proposes a reform of teaching methods based upon a revised set of ideas about children's learning.

We should learn from what the best teachers have always done, and in future plan the enjoyment and involvement of all pupils in the part of life they spend in our care. The claim that youngsters can become active citizens, deciding together matters previously left to leaders and specialists, can eventually be justified only by the enterprise of teachers and the success of ideas for improving the way we learn at school.

Introduction: the idea of a common school

Few teachers and fewer parents can say why children should go to comprehensive rather than to grammar schools or describe the distinctive features of an all-ability education. In the early days radicals wanted to open the doors of the academic system, not to change it, and campaigned for equal opportunities for all children and an end to premature selection. In consequence change has been administrative rather than philosophical, with teachers' habits and instincts proving more influential than any reform agenda. Reorganisation has produced an incomplete patchwork of local compromises so that at almost every age between five and eighteen there are pupils somewhere in the country transferring from one type of school to another. The notion of a common education with new possibilities for teaching and learning has been all but lost in local independence and diversity.

Politicians, teachers and administrators concerned with building and managing common schools have seldom ventured away from the orthodox path of professional discourse. Far from devising a plan for comprehensive education, the pioneers began by making grammar school courses more freely available. At a crucial stage the issue of physical access to lessons overshadowed questions of content and method. It is as if equality of opportunity were an end in itself, as if common schools were made by the simple fact of admission. In the absence of a redefinition of the aims of education the reorganised schools are seen by most pupils, teachers and parents as a ladder of advancement for individuals. Children are told to work hard, earn qualifications and to expect their job prospects to be enhanced proportionately. In response to a once expanding economy and to the pressure of examination boards, themselves influenced by ever-greater demands for qualifications, teachers have developed a competitive, meritocratic model of education. The focus of teaching, learning and success is the individual, so that differences between children seem to be of fundamental importance.

Tell-tale words and phrases like 'less able', 'academic', 'bright' or 'practically minded' reflect the persistence in teachers' minds of pre-comprehensive stereotypes of children. Youngsters are divided by elaborate assessment procedures according to their apparently innate propensity for learning, so that their experiences of school are quite various. The result is a utilitarian, market-place pluralism through which individual merit or brightness is supposedly advanced. Cultural influences on children's language and attitudes are recognised but only exceptionally influence teaching. Writing and copying in formal, standard English dominates the curriculum,[1] and teachers seem to be engaged in reproducing their own culture and values.

Individualism and meritocracy

Subject specialisation reinforces this concern for individuals. Children learn by picking up pebbles from a beach rather than by sharing a growing web of experiences. Each pebble has an assigned value or status and the pupils whose natural merit enables them to select an adequate number of stones hope for power and income for life. Their contribution is forever afterwards valued on a different scale. The more numerous remainder is left with some well-worn shingle that may be useful later. As early as 1958 Michael Young offered a satirical commentary on this emerging philosophy:

Till the middle of the century practical socialists identified
equality with advancement for merit . . . The planners were
(happily for posterity) terrified by the kind of criticism fired at
them by the grammar schools . . . They imported old principles into new framework and made the core of the comprehensive not so much a common curriculum as a miniature
grammar school. They made a grammar school first and added
on the other bits later . . . The interests of the clever children
came first . . . Obviously it would have been wrong to place
the bright children in the same class as the dull, for then the
former would have been held back to the pace of the slowest. In
practice, the comprehensive schools, by dividing the goats
from the sheep, continued to abide by the segregation of ability
which was the saving grace of the whole educational system.[2]

Young's success in anticipating the behaviour of comprehensive schools suggests a certain inevitability about the persistence of previous traditions of schooling. In the absence of a
coherent and distinct philosophy of democratic education
there was no realistic alternative. The implications of the
failure to devise new objectives were clear to Young in 1958:

Today we frankly recognise that democracy can be no more
than aspiration, and have rule not so much by the people as by
the cleverest people; not an aristocracy of birth, not a plutoc-
racy of wealth, but a true meritocracy of talent.[3]

Teachers should not be comfortable with the realisation that
the whole history of common schools could have been written
in advance.

The classic statement of the case for concentrating on
individuals is Samuel Smiles's *Self-Help*, first published in
1859. Smiles, like Adam Smith, believed that the efforts of
individuals could only enrich the commonweal. As he put it in
his first chapter:

National progress is the sum of individual industry, energy,
and uprightness, as national decay is of individual idleness,
selfishness, and vice . . . The greatest slave is not he who is
ruled by a despot, great though that evil be, but he who is the
thrall of his own moral ignorance, selfishness and vice . . . The
solid foundations of liberty must rest upon individual character; which is also the only sure guarantee for social security and
national progress . . . It is this energy of individual life and

example acting throughout society, which constitutes the best practical education of Englishmen. Schools, academies, and colleges, give but the merest beginnings of culture in comparison with it.[4]

Self-Help, and the theory that it publicised, begs the social question in several directions at once. It is pleasant to think of strong-willed individuals surmounting the disadvantages of family and fortune in heroic style, natural merit winning through. While modern sociology has not solved the conundrum of culture and character it has identified some uncomfortable correlations between behaviour and circumstances. Unemployment seems to breed passivity even if not all the unemployed are apathetic; there are predictable features in the family environment of delinquents. Reformers should not expect too much from an individual character that is itself the result of other social influences. If people are malleable, responsive to experiences of every kind and perhaps permanently afflicted by deprivation or trauma, who can be certain that apparent merit is not reflected good fortune?

In a complex modern state there are real dangers in fostering the increasingly specialised strivings of individuals. People are differentiated and divided so that instead of a 'guarantee for social security' there is a collection of hyperactive meritocrats ministering to the needs of the passive remnant. Everything from government to snooker becomes a business for professionals and experts. Schools, which might be communities with hope of social cohesion and integration, become instruments of manpower planning in a free society, contributing to cities of isolated nuclear families. Education based on merit and differences encourages pupils to view life as a game of careers, an escalator from the classroom to the professions and beyond. Learning and knowledge come to have value only as an applied art of self-advancement.

Individualist ideas were in tune with the pre-comprehensive pattern of heterogeneous schools adapted to the supposed needs of various defined 'types' of pupil, but such notions compromise the basis for a common education before it has begun. However meritocratic theory is applied it cannot lead, by definition, to material success for more than a small number of pupils. Comprehensives are no more able to arrange for everyone to win prizes than were the grammar schools before them; in attempting to do so, they raise expectations only to dash them again. If it is agreed that differences between pupils should lead to a diverse teaching programme, why bring them together in the first place? Why create schools so large and variegated that only sophisticated timetables can match children and resources efficiently?

Improvement and civility

For want of anything better, some Headteachers have made a virtue of size and complexity, explaining how well comprehensives have imitated their predecessors. Attempts to evade the question 'What for?' by presenting examination results in a favourable light have not convinced a sceptical public. As there is no distinctive image or idea of what common schools are about, their success can be measured only by the criteria of their rivals. Such comparisons, invidious though they are, have made it fashionable once more to speak of grammar schools as agents of working-class progress, to hint that comprehensives have betrayed high standards and civilised values in pursuit of social engineering.

To some extent this failure to define the nature and purpose of a common education stems from a preoccupation with social improvement. Mass education has seemed to be about 'levelling up' the dispossessed rather than finding a form of learning able to bring everyone together. After the passage of the 1867 Reform Bill, Robert Lowe remarked that it was essential 'to compel our future masters to learn their letters'.[5] He feared brute ignorance sweeping aside the enlightened government of the best, and hoped that if the masses were familiar with the alphabet they might also be fit to give the assent of the governed. Reluctant reformers argued that the state had now a responsibility to civilise the working classes. Robert Owen, for all his reputation as a friend of labour, shared many of Lowe's anxieties. His *New View of Society* can be read as an attempt to impose social discipline, to fit children for tasks prescribed by others. He argues, for example, that:

. . . the outline of our future proceedings then becomes clear
and defined . . . They direct that the governing powers of all
countries should establish rational plans for the education and
general formation of the characters of their subjects. These
plans must be devised to train children from their earliest
infancy in good habits of every description (which will of
course prevent them from acquiring those of falsehood and
deception). They must afterwards be rationally educated, and
their labour be usefully directed.[6]

Owen's scheme was manipulative in the extreme, unconsciously designed to extirpate a working-class culture that
seemed unsavoury and uncivilised from the social distance
then existing between government and people. Modern radicals write in an opposite sense, as if on behalf of a poor whose
natural rights have been removed by a supposed middle-class
conspiracy. The effect is the same: public education has been
planned by one group of people and is experienced by another;
the masses have been imagined as subjects suitable for reform.
This condescending frame of mind is not one in which learning is properly understood.

   George Orwell's advice to himself as a social explorer is
equally relevant for teachers inclined to patronise their pupils:

It is no use clapping a proletarian on the back and telling him
that he is as good a man as I am; if I want real contact with him,
I have got to make an effort for which very likely I am
unprepared. For to get outside the class racket I have got to
suppress not merely my private snobbishness, but most of my
other tastes and prejudices as well. I have got to alter myself so
completely that at the end I should hardly be recognisable as the
same person. What is involved is not merely the amelioration
of working-class conditions, nor an avoidance of the more
stupid forms of snobbery, but a complete abandonment of the
upper-class and middle-class attitude to life. And whether I say
Yes or No probably depends upon the extent to which I grasp
what is demanded of me.[7]

Injustice and democracy

Comprehensive schools are not simply or mainly about the
working classes, underprivilege or relative disadvantage, im-

portant though it is to redress the balance of past injustice. Great possibilities were opened for a new generation by the abolition of the eleven-plus examination; but a convincingly comprehensive critique of traditional, divisive forms of education would surely be unaltered even if every 'able' child had always enjoyed a guaranteed place in a public or grammar school. The inescapable claim of the comprehensive is that all children, of whatever ability or background, should be educated together and will benefit profoundly from the shared experience. People whose families have always had access to academic education also need to value the special qualities of a common school and appreciate that they too have been disadvantaged by selection and its consequences. This is unlikely to happen while comprehensive classrooms persist in an 'economy' version of traditional teaching and fail to develop their unique potential.

The comprehensive experience has suffered from its accidental beginnings as a rebellion against the eleven-plus. Teachers were left to work out for themselves the consequences of a fragmented revolution without an acknowledged prophet or manifesto. Once all the children of a neighbourhood were grouped together under one roof, however, the *educational* deficiencies of the misconceived grammar school enterprise were exposed. Faced with the diverse turmoil of divided schools, Heads and teachers have slowly recognised that selection and differentiation were damaging the very fabric of society, diminishing the human value of all children, alleged successes and failures alike. In recent years teachers have begun to discover that a sense of community, a simple togetherness, has educational as well as social implications. The image of cooperation and mutuality has been contrasted with competitive individualism and has suggested an alternative definition of learning as well as new strategies for organising and presenting lessons.

Formal, abstract and literary activity that once passed for learning seems deeply unsatisfactory if an individual's development and success are seen to depend upon unfolding relationships and a network of living experiences. The comprehensive assumption is that children cannot grow naturally in isolation from one another, that membership of the community and neighbourhood is central to achieving a fully human condition. Schools where the preoccupation is the health of society and groups rather than individual progress will be concerned to foster the arts of democracy and self-government rather than technical, vocational skills or the narrow understanding of the specialist.

After 1945, when the desire for a less socially divided, more educated and more democratic Britain was strong, Aneurin Bevan focused upon the reciprocal connection between knowledge and power, insisting on the link between education and democracy, learning and self-government:

> . . . for the first time in history the common man steps on the stage. We insist that education is primarily concerned with the ordinary person, and not with the exceptional person. The ordinary person is asked to decide issues of far greater gravity than any exceptional person in the past . . . When I complain about our secondary schools imitating the public schools it is because they have a different task to perform . . . In order to be on terms of equality with the product of the public schools they must be trained differently. They are already too much inclined to obedience. What we want for them is more arrogance, freedom from the trammels of tradition. These boys and girls are to be asked to wield the royal sceptre; we must therefore give them the souls of kings and queens. Otherwise it may be said of us that we took the ordinary man from the shadows of history and set him in the fierce light that beats upon thrones and he was blinded and ran away.[8]

Bevan recognised, as Labour's more expert advisory committee policy-makers did not, that public education could not succeed by simply extending grammar or independent opportunities to everyone. For him the common school would be the first to offer all pupils access to citizenship and self-government; to succeed would need an original curriculum and method. He confidently believed in mass democracy because he sensed that ordinary people could learn the business of government and how to manage the affairs of their communities.

Bevan came from outside the established institutions of merit and was unimpressed by the 'excellence' or talent of those who, in his day, attempted to monopolise power and decision-making. He was rare in demanding that working people should be princes and princesses, active in their own learning, raised to exercise power. He saw that the judgement of ordinary men and women might be as valid as that of the clever, and suspected that political intelligence might not be confined to the political élite. Learning for Bevan meant practice with the royal sceptre; it is the process by which we understand ourselves in relation to others and come to accept responsibility for our own lives. Democracy has to be alive with everyone involved because otherwise the specialists will take decisions for us, restoring in meritocratic clothing the powerless condition of ignorant subjects.

This book is an attempt to extend and redefine the idea of common education from this perspective. It seeks to establish the proposition that children learn best when they work together and that their similarities as citizens of a democratic society are of much greater importance than their differences as individuals. The implication for schools of this renewed emphasis upon groups and relationships as a source of knowledge and understanding is then explored. Learning is described here as the fruit of relations between children and their experiences, not as the application of the intrinsic ability of individuals to abstract problems. All children not most severely handicapped have sufficient ability to justify schools basing their work upon the prospect of cooperative citizenship for everyone. These ideas open the way for the changes in management, curriculum, teaching and assessment necessary to create a distinctive, authentically comprehensive pattern of education and a more democratic society.

Such a definition is crucial if the potential learning community implicit in the common school is to be realised, but proposals for changed practice must be related to the present state of the experiment. What has been achieved so far? What images of school and notions of learning influence teachers and parents?

CHAPTER 1

The comprehensive experience today

Everyone, including today members of the Royal family, has been to school. Most of those who, for one reason or another, debate education also have children 'in the system'. People have an inbuilt insider's knowledge of the classroom compared with which their awareness of other institutions is negligible. The public may have a grievance about the workings of hospitals or law courts, but it does not, on the whole, accumulate 15,000 hours of practical, personal experience supported by a folk memory drawn on several generations. This reservoir of understanding coexists with popular images of school derived from myth or hysteria.

Neither *Tom Brown's Schooldays* nor *Grange Hill* have much to do with the reality of education in suburban England, but there is a psychological truth about the escapades of schoolroom rebels. Pupils remember the ineffectual teachers who created an unselfconscious anarchy in the normally tightly controlled spaces of the classroom. Tales of disorder, vandalism, sexual misconduct and disaster retain their credibility however absurd or untypical they are known to be. There is an incipient, Evelyn-Waugh-like farce in the public theatre of assembly hall, study or lesson; a barely repressed comedy of authority that writers or television producers soon craft into entertainment. The crumbling fabric of a poor lesson, its lunacy recalled with an hilarity that disguises an inner fear of chaos, becomes the 'scandal' of comprehensive education. It is less often remembered that concealed beneath the grey stones of more naturally prestigious schools lurk equally desperate characters in search of order. Demos has no monopoly on eccentricity.

The search for status

The myth of school serves other needs, however, reflecting an urgent desire for security and a sense of belonging. Modern housing developments have converted town and country into a continuous suburbia where traditional social patterns are transformed. Daily personal relations of the kind necessary for deference are rare; even the doctor operates from a group practice or health centre, while priests have become invisible and ecumenical. Work that confers status is remote from homes that are somehow inadequate to express the feelings of their inhabitants. No home extension, no manicured lawn, no symbolism of gate-post or door-knob can convey sufficiently the meaning of a family's life. What is the point of drawing a suburban family tree if it turns out that the Appleyards have antecedents no more interesting than themselves? This is not mere snobbery but a search for permanence, for tradition, for a private history substantial enough to leave its mark upon the pebble-dashed landscape of mass society. People want any-thing but a collective, uniform existence; they instinctively reject the municipal style whenever there is an alternative. Timber and brick, however phoney their Jacobean/Tudor masquerade, are seen as natural and authentic materials in-finitely to be preferred to concrete and steel.

    Public and grammar schools draw their strength from this anxious search for meaning, for a fabric of life that has always been there, for stone, lawns, hedges, trees and an ancient house, for an enclosed order within which everyone has a place. When teachers complain of their own lost 'standing in the community' they articulate only the common sadness of an increasingly suburban population.

This understandable desire to be associated with tradition and painfully acquired maturity inevitably leads to myth as it is an inescapable fact that there are not enough grey stones to go round. Only twenty or thirty schools in the United Kingdom have a 'history worth writing about' or possess buildings in themselves redolent of ancient scholarship. To compensate for such 'deficiencies' many a glossy brochure seeks to create in parental minds associations rich enough to substitute for reality. 'Ancient' is, from an advertiser's standpoint, as flexible as 'sea view'. Parents with money to spend look for these powerful images just as they might examine the furniture and fittings of a restaurant before ordering a meal. You cannot eat candles or reproduction scrolled table-legs but they excite expectations sufficient to make an average dinner memorable. 'Class' is assumed to be expensive, and good teachers are thought to be as rare and desirable as plovers' eggs or asparagus tips. Private education is like perfume; the customer's desire is heightened by the price tag, and the fragrance of the product is enhanced by a carefully cultivated atmosphere of exclusiveness. How can children fail if they have parents who believe education is worth paying for?

Meanwhile, a great many parents have no choice at all. Every secondary school in Britain can promise spats and top hats for all, or even for the hard-working, but exclusiveness cannot be democratised without losing its appeal. If excellence in education is defined in grammar or public school terms it will clearly remain unavailable for the great majority of citizens. The legends of Eton, Harrow, Marlborough and Rugby are so seductively attractive, however, that they continue to influence, even determine, the purposes of secondary education. In consequence the neighbourhood school is bound to fail in a race for which it should not have been entered, and is judged by umpires and journalists who grew up with Frank Richards and the Eton Boating Song.

Unlike Aneurin Bevan, planners of the comprehensive school did not make this analysis or arrive at these conclusions. Harold Wilson, whose administrations will be remembered mainly for establishing the comprehensive system with the consent of most local authorities, could himself see no further than grammar schools all round. An understanding of

comprehensives and their reception should begin in this public school world, at the roots of English images of education.
Without an appraisal of the 'world we have lost' and the
schools that have succeeded them, a forlorn pursuit of examination certificates and career advancement for all is irresist-
ible. Comprehensive schools do not make sense until their
distinctive purposes and methods are made clear.

The whole point of a public or grammar school is that as
soon as pupils enter the gate they feel part of a unique, special
institution quite unlike anything at home. Membership reinforces their self-esteem even when they have still to learn the
hallowed rituals and unfamiliar vocabulary. There are very
few purpose-built comprehensives but in cities where these
exist the imagery is of factories and mass production. Glass,
steel and concrete suggest a brief but geometric life without
privacy. London's comprehensives, for example, were
planned in the aftermath of the Festival of Britain; futuristic
sculpture and marble staircases were the visual focus of vast
palaces – Kidbrooke, Eltham Green, Crown Woods, Forest
Hill – each confidently designed to accommodate two
thousand or more children. It was the same period and reflex as
the tower block, a triumphant seizure of the initiative by the
modern movement, filling a vacuum in postwar London with
architecture anticipating lunar exploration and space stations.
It was the same visual world as Dan Dare in the *Eagle* comic.

This confidence and excitement had its own attractions,
particularly for young teachers and some pupils. For parents
the appeal was less. Hardly any pupil *chose* a comprehensive;
they were directed to vacant places. How could children
survive such crowded playgrounds and corridors? What about
the offer of a place at Dulwich College or Roan, or Shooters
Hill or Colfe's? Would it be fair to Tom Brown to commit him
to the care of this 'brave new world'? Perhaps the schools were
special in a sense but they did not make their pupils special.
The popular and local press described the early comprehensives as creating uniformity, 'levelling down', 'making everyone the same'. The eleven-plus and the grammar school
offered a privilege ticket to an exclusive club; the comprehensive was presented as a seething morass from which only the
most competitive and determined would emerge. Ambitious

parents and children who had no choice recognised in the comprehensives a galaxy of opportunities and made such schools their own. 'Grammar schools for all', 'equality of opportunity' and a 'fair deal for all our children' became potent slogans appealing to aspiring families who resented the charmed circle of an establishment that suddenly seemed vulnerable. The great mass of parents sent their children to school, not apathetically but uncritically. They wanted something better for their offspring but not to the extent of arguing or complaining.

As reorganisation proceeded in the 1960s and 1970s many comprehensives were created that were anything but purpose-built. Some were enlarged secondary moderns; catchment areas meant many schools retained much of their former character. Split-site schools and a host of different local arrangements did not suggest either confidence or excitement. Teachers were often reluctant, particularly those in grammar schools who feared what ordinary children might be like. Parents were equally apprehensive of the social melting pot. Grammar schools had been engines of status for everyone connected with them and, unlike private education, cost their customers nothing. By contrast the new schools in their very nature could offer their pupils no distinction, no sense of being special or somehow having been 'chosen' for better things. Indeed, the very phrase 'equality of opportunity' implied that everything was still to be played for. The argument that children of able or aspiring parents would succeed just as before, or that the welfare state would benefit active rather than passive citizens, was too sophisticated for the time, or for the feelings shared by many people, now deprived of a cherished institution, the relative modernity of which in many towns was conveniently forgotten. The continued existence of the fee-paying alternative, and of grammar schools in some trenchant authorities, also meant that the comprehensive was in danger of seeming a 'low status' rather than a 'no status' option.

This struggle for status and acceptance has profoundly affected the development and nature of the reorganised schools and has in effect committed comprehensives to an impossible task. Higher status (whether intellectual or social) and better careers are not available on a mass basis; schools can influence the *distribution* of 'life chances', not their absolute number. And yet comprehensive schools have been driven to compete in these terms, seeking status and credibility through their examination results. It is a sad irony that the grammar school, with its pathetic record of B- and C-stream failure and narrow curriculum, enjoyed a warm glow of approval and respect without such efforts. Grammar and public school failure is different because it is respectable. The disaffected or unsuccessful pupil at an independent school does not also face a life of social rejection, unemployment or drudgery.

It is, nevertheless, easy to understand how comprehensive schools set off up this handsome blind alley, neglecting to develop a distinctive educational strategy, preferring instead an instrumental model of learning in which everyone competes for medals, certificates and 'good jobs'. Teachers clung to what they knew; many of them had not asked to be employed in comprehensives. Heads wanted to prove that comprehensives were every bit as good as their rivals; parents had to be wooed and the school's reputation was at stake in the market place. Status was what almost everyone wanted, but no one noticed, or perhaps people did not wish to notice, that status is by definition individious and certainly irrelevant to the purposes of democratic education. So began the ever-improving examination results, the litany of competitive successes, the catalogue of Oxbridge awards and university places. Most pervasive of all was the sense that these successes and victories were individual, reflecting glory on alma mater no doubt, but individual in their merit and purpose. The dim and the slow were, of course, to be inspired as well as filled with admiration.

Unchosen children

Pupils are selected for comprehensive school by accidents of social geography. Teachers are expected to succeed with an arbitrary and random collection of children. For all the fear of uniformity, there is a remarkable diversity in the handicaps from which people can suffer and which teachers must accept.

Children from tower blocks; children with sick and disabled parents; children on free meals; children of the unemployed; children with reading ages of up to five years behind their chronological age; children of night workers; children of shift workers; children themselves working for supermarkets or newsagents; stepchildren: thousands of unattractively packaged, unsuccessful children whose efforts can be condemned or sneered at by sharp-eyed journalists and politicians as evidence of comprehensive failure. Eighty per cent do not pass Ordinary ('O') level of the General Certificate of Education (GCE); hardly any sit Advanced ('A') level or go to university. Fewer still become lawyers, civil servants, members of Parliament, doctors, clergymen, or even teachers. Most end up, or used to end up, in manual or minor clerical occupations similar to those of their families. That, after all, is what most people do. Now it is the dole instead of drudgery. In such a world of non-accomplishment, self-esteem and self-confidence are rare and infinitely precious; children assume themselves to be deficient in essential human attributes and accept the justice of their own placing in society. Does it matter, for pupils like these, whether the curriculum is technical, academic, liberal, relevant or irrelevant? Clearly not if the aim is bright-faced public school lookalikes, alive with a sense of their own importance and equipped for a career of steadily unfolding success and ever-increasing status.

By contrast, pupils whose parents own shares, manage businesses, run banks, judge law suits, site oil wells, invent computer systems, render advice to ministers, design buildings, write for national newspapers, teach at universities, command soldiers or ships, fly planes, deal in stocks or render accounts are not well represented. The typical neighbourhood school in an industrial city has a compressed social range from which many of the wealthy and ambitious have excluded themselves. An indication of the extent of this self-exclusion is the fact that while only 5 per cent of the population attends independent schools, 25 per cent of the places in universities go to pupils from the private education sector. The concentration of wealthier parents in particular areas, the operation of the assisted places scheme and the surviving grammar schools further ensure a secret and unacknowledged 'creaming' process. A comprehensive system does not exist; but even if it did, it could not deliver success in the terms of the grammar/public school myth.

As it is, incomplete comprehensive schools and an incomplete system are criticised for failing to flatten the social pyramid or failing to confer the privileges of the upper echelons of the hierarchy upon everyone. The widespread criticism of schools is only plausible because teachers sometimes seem to be attempting something of this nature, a doomed labour of Hercules. As a result they stand accused of converting a sow's ear into a sow's ear, indeed of manufacturing the wretched ear in the first place. The attack has been focused on secondary schooling, and the blows have been hard.

It is interesting to speculate why primary schools have been less stringently appraised despite the William Tyndale débâcle, tending to enjoy greater public confidence. Part of this is a question of distance. Who can blame a first school for the quality of school leavers? Secondaries also suffer from the unappealing age and habits of their pupils. The raising of the school-leaving age set many more problems than secondary reorganisation which, in many areas, coincided with the 'extra year'. At seven or eight, eagerness and vitality have not been obscured by the group activities of a self-conscious, pubescent teenager. Anomie and adolescence have a good deal in common. On the other hand, primary schools have to some extent been romanticised, by teachers in senior schools as much as by parents or press. It is easy to visualise keen young children trembling with excitement and new ideas.

Where has this vitality gone by the time children are twelve or thirteen? Some secondary schools are tempted to organise their first and second years on primary lines with fewer teachers and less specialisation, partly to secure continuity but also in pursuit of a dream. Failure and alienation do not begin at eleven. If they did how is it that reading ages vary almost from the point at which reading begins? What is the maximum difference in vocabulary at age seven between children who later enjoy and succeed at specialised, so-called 'academic' subjects and those who do not? The truth is that most children enter secondary school with a very clear sense of self and a substantial prehistory of success or failure. This is not an attempt to criticise primary teachers or to shift the burden of responsibility, only to point out that trees have roots. Often the roots of low self-esteem have very little to do with school at all; well-loved children have a light in their eyes that cannot be extinguished by any subsequent learning difficulty and that in itself seems to make problems less likely.

Youth can seem to threaten adults and their world. However well integrated and adjusted schools become they will still be inhabited by acne'd young men and women who prefer jeans and 'rock' to blazers and Beethoven, who enjoy sexual experimentation more than homework. In the second-ary years, emotions, relationships and friendships become increasingly important and complex. The question of personal identity is asked to the point of crisis and the last thing a reasonable, healthy youngster wants to do is to spend long evenings in secluded study. At the same time as they are asked to sit examinations many fourteen- or fifteen-year-olds find themselves cut off from or in conflict with their parents. There is the battle to stake out independent territory in a confined home, worries about clothes and personal appearance, eventu-ally fear of failure and unemployment. Secondary schools are as easy to attack or dislike as young people themselves.

In these circumstances there is a striking, stubborn am-bition about Heads and teachers who have entered the free market economy of parental choice preaching success for all. With an almost Victorian belief in progress and self-improvement, comprehensive schools have scaled the Heights of Abraham with meagre equipment and very few advantages. It is surprising that teachers remain optimistic about their prospects of success. Schools give the impression that they are but a few steps from their objectives. It is as if teachers had undertaken to reverse social history in those 15,000 hours.

A time factor

State schools attempt such heroic tasks without an important advantage possessed by their private rivals. At the apex of the English system the great public schools have twenty-four hours a day to form the minds and character of pupils often already endowed with every advantage of wealth and parental support. Meanwhile the vast remainder, of whom politicians and public expect so much, are supposed to be transformed in a mere five hours daily. Most pupils at independent schools do not board, but the image of boarding shapes public perceptions of the contrast between private and maintained schools; this helps to illustrate what comprehensive teachers are about. A boy or girl sent away to school has a profoundly different experience from the rest; day schools of whatever alleged character have much more in common than their clients would believe, so entrenched is the myth. Variations in the quality of lessons are related to the individual teacher, not to schools or institutions.

Boarding has a culture of its own not easily written about by an outsider. When the social damage attributed to divorce, one-parent families and women at work is calculated generations of public school semi-orphans are forgotten. Sending a seven-year-old away to school is an extraordinary act and depends upon the sanction of family habit as well as a class solidarity as intense as that of a Welsh mining village. The family interest is partly sacrificed to the ideal of an élite with an ascendancy so automatic as to amount to a tradition of public service. For the child a total, almost totalitarian, experience is substituted for the fragmentary and episodic character of the school–home dialogue. Orwell learned about Big Brother at St Cyprians, although the writer possibly invented as many features of his prep school as he did of *Nineteen Eighty-four*. The bizarre public school voice, the identikit manners, the sporting types: these could be created only by a total institution where the individuals are slowly and perhaps painfully assimilated by a process in which every detail of their existence is planned for them.

No day school could imitate such a pattern, least of all a comprehensive with its jumbled social roots. Teachers can speak of 'care' but it is an emotion somewhat circumscribed by the time available. Day school teachers can aspire to achieve the influence of a Jean Brodie but their scope for the Jesuitical possession of a child's mind and body is strictly limited. The teaching service has been professionalised, adopting all the conscientious detachment that implies, but time is the crucial difference. The existence and relations of the pupils are as contrasted in day and boarding schools as they are in civilian and army life.

A comprehensive cannot achieve the intensity, cohesion and solidarity of boarding. All the most essential parts of school (private reading and writing, sport, music and entertainment) become voluntary, extracurricular activities. The coercion of one becomes the bluff of the other. Boarding schools are, by their nature, small and socially homogeneous; their objectives are narrow where they are not defined by accepted tradition. Their values and destinations fall within easily defined limits of respectability. A boarding school existence from age seven to eighteen can make a profound difference in a way that cannot be matched by all those hours of compulsory education. The preparatory-aged pupil living in a suburban house probably watches television for a longer period than he spends with his teachers. Since 1979 the progressive withdrawal of milk and meals subsidies has further reduced the coherence and sociability of maintained schools. Fish-and-chips at a corner shop does not contribute much to the communality of school. Teachers have increasingly withdrawn from non-lesson-time activities as industrial disputes have succeeded one another. This is a further symptom of the 'professionalisation' of teaching; many staff would prefer to teach on the French model – delivering lessons like lectures and otherwise disconnecting themselves from the corporate life of the school. Teaching contracts with specific duties listed would only ratify a growing tendency to retreat from the imitation of public school models already fairly threadbare. Such reflections further underline the ambition and difficulty of the comprehensive experiment and the noble folly of great expectations.

Teachers

None of the contrasts between comprehensive schools and their predecessors examined above matters as much as the individual teachers who comprise the real message of education, however it is organised. In this teacher element, schools are most alike; here, stereotypes and generalisations are least helpful. A master at Eton is a world away from Eltham Green in his social attitudes and assumptions, in his career pattern and in his private expectations of life. In the classroom, however, he is a teacher preparing students for the same examinations as his comprehensive counterpart using similar books and resources. The homogeneity and concentration of higher education in England exercise a silent unifying influence upon the nation's school system and culture. The rise of Science, the decline of the Classics and the development of a common curriculum *within* reorganised schools have contributed to this growing convergence. Whichever school disinterested observers enter they will find many of the same activities and subjects. There are few schools without almost all the major academic disciplines. Chemistry, Physics, Art, Craft and Foreign Languages are more or less universal and the insecurity of a grammar school woodworker or a secondary modern linguist has more or less disappeared. Public schools sometimes have more equipment and a better pupil–teacher ratio but the substance of their offering is indistinguishable in any important respect from that of other places.

It is not just a question of a faithful reprint of a classic pattern. The public schools themselves have discovered Science, Technology, Art and Craft as well as losing confidence in Ancient Languages and a rigid Arts/Science divide. Economics, Sociology and other new subjects have spread with equal rapidity in independent and maintained sectors. All schools have been victims or beneficiaries of the post-war liberalisation of university curricula. There is no evidence at all that public school teachers have better qualifications or teach more effectively than those employed by local authorities. There are almost certainly as many variations within the private sector or within any school as there are between one type of school and another.

Despite this remarkable convergence almost anyone could tell the difference between the staffroom of an independent school and that of its comprehensive neighbour. The style, the tone of voice and the atmosphere of the masters' common room in a fee-paying school is instantly recognisable but the influence of such factors on the nature and content of teaching is strikingly small. Key words and phrases almost taste of what they signify: 'masters and mistresses'/'teachers', 'common room'/'staffroom', 'boys' and girls'/'kids'. The messages are social rather than educational in content.

There is a danger in any generalisation about teachers (a most numerous profession), but despite rapid changes since 1945 public school staff have remained a distinctive and relatively homogeneous body, well-bred adults in a private world. They were, in their own time, boarders; for them the enclosed order of college and quadrangle, chapel and cloister (even where these are imaginary), is relatively undisturbed: their social assumptions and prejudices are untested by facts. For them the armed forces, the ancient universities and the Church have a reality and importance undreamt of on a Wimpey estate. Teachers at the better known schools are very much of George Orwell's 'lower upper middle class'; born into the professions, untainted by industrial life, eventually suburban but possessed by an image of the English country-side and character that belongs to John Betjeman and the 1930s and is all the more attractive for that. Some of these teachers are gifted scholars, a vague echo of the days when clergymen, Oxbridge fellows and housemasters in public schools were part of an interchangeable freemasonry of Cricket and Classics. The inbred quality of this élite gives it the flavour of a closed circle, self-selecting and self-approving.

The superficial egalitarianism of the Wilson years raised many questions for the public school. It often surprised out-siders that 'masters' and 'mistresses' were not more con-science-stricken at their separate and privileged existence.[1] The absence of any internal doubt or debate is a clear evidence of the predominantly social character of independent school-ing. People born and bred into certain habits and traditions are likely to question advantages only when they cease to be advantageous. The disapproval of a Hampstead intellectual or a trade union convener will not induce guilt amongst those whose experience is that 'simply everyone' goes to private school. A great many independent schools (particularly of a preparatory kind) are inferior and do not achieve the style or tone described here, making do with unqualified or under-qualified teachers and lacking the resources to rival the maintained sector. A private school is an expensive undertaking. Some have no more substance than pasteboard nostalgia for a departed era, but the underlying social spirit and attitude amongst the teachers are similar to those of more exclusive versions.

The cult of the clever pupil is often an important elaboration of the self-conscious superiority sketched above. Keen young adults, themselves well spoken and fresh from a liberal university education, hasten to the presumed groves of academe where they scent the chance to manufacture their own image, a cultivated and elegant cleverness unsullied by coarse minds or people. Plato's *déjeuner sur l'herbe* seems to be the arcadian model for male educational relationships in which masters 'influence' boys who hope to be leading figures in the next generation. Social and intellectual identities become subtly confused in a mutually flattering and cultured discourse. For an outsider the public school world remains suffocating, mysterious and immensely self-confident. The only unease felt by the staff is the faint sense that many pupils are their social superiors.

The milieu of the comprehensive staffroom is in sharp contrast to this portrait. There are large numbers of women, almost no ex-public school-boys, hardly any Oxbridge graduates, little connection with the Church or services and a striking diversity of backgrounds and expertise. Patterns can be detected (mainly of the 'lower middle-class', 'suburban grammar school' type) but despite complex and largely uncharted social origins and diffuse influences from previous traditions of schooling, comprehensives have created their own original atmosphere and unity of purpose. The ghosts of 'grammar' and 'secondary modern' traditions of teaching have had their influence, but many comprehensives now have had a history of up to a quarter of a century in which to develop their own style.

Staff and pupil turnover in the last ten years have been sufficient to dilute if not eliminate images and approaches derived from other forms of school. Non-graduate teachers were more likely to accept 'pastoral' posts on reorganisation; since then the profession, the schools and even many of the individuals have moved on. Teaching is becoming an 'all graduate' business; Heads do not appoint less qualified staff to safeguard a school's pastoral future. Qualities of character and personality as well as individual interests and opportunities are more likely to shape career patterns within a school.

Subjects do not carry an automatic status; good and bad teaching are the essential ingredients of a department's reputation. Home Economics, PE and Art may struggle for parental esteem; indeed, only English, Mathematics and Science enjoy complete public acceptance; inside the schools, however, teachers are valued for what they do, not for where they came from or what subject they teach. No subject or qualification is a barrier to promotion in itself. The development of a common curriculum means that no department (except the remedial) is naturally associated with slow learners or more able students; in consequence a parity of esteem is possible. Increased participation in examinations (especially since the raising of the school-leaving age) has had a similar effect. Art and Woodwork can contribute to the flow of 'results' as happily as Science or History. Staffrooms are much less interested in the qualifications of colleagues than was once the case; part of this is the effect of the Open University and the B.Ed. degree in equalising teachers' professional standing, but it is also evidence of an acceptance that all subjects have a rightful place in a broad curriculum.

Comprehensive teachers are natural members of the increasingly white-collar communities they serve, very often providing leadership in a wide range of activities. Few feel socially or intellectually ill at ease with parents or pupils. A teacher's values, like those of suburban society itself, are often inexplicit. Informal, relaxed relationships and behaviour disguise moral, political or religious tensions. Teachers are as ambiguous as their neighbours. This does not mean that teachers have disclaimed ideas or prejudice, but the open, vague contemporary atmosphere makes the definition of a school and its purpose a tricky business. Headteachers have to discover and express a philosophy that focuses their work without offending the diverse opinions of staff and parents. Outward details like uniform become disproportionately significant, standing for a common identity and perhaps offering reassurance. Where schools have trouble in projecting an image or identity, success is more difficult to achieve. Schools cannot afford to be too many things to too many people.

Pupils' social experiences

Important though adult perceptions are, it is children who are, in Peter Dawson's phrase, 'making comprehensives work'.[2] Pupils rather than teachers are the main source and cause of differences between one school and another and it is their experience that is central to an evaluation of the comprehensive experience. Staff do not always appreciate that the most effective means of creating a favourable public image is to teach well; parents move more slowly than their children but the relayed muddled story is as potent as any well-produced Headteacher's letter.

For the pupils, school is a huge overplayed melodrama of heroes and villains in which fear, excitement and boredom are mixed in reasonably equal proportions. 'Will I know where to go?' 'Will my head be stuck down the lavatory pan?' 'Will I be able to cope with the work?' 'Will I make friends?' they ask on the first day. There is a physical and emotional intensity about a school that stems from its role as the largest community to which its members belong. Halls and corridors bursting with young people can seem to the newcomer both threatening and exhilarating, the sharpest possible contrast to domestic solitude. Between lessons and at break-times many schools, particularly those on several floors, present a congested, busy scene similar to a shopping arcade on a Saturday afternoon. The spectacle of a seething corridor is the image that haunts the imagination of those who dislike large schools. Children, however, behave better than adults would in similar circumstances, perhaps because they are younger and less sensitive to physical contact.

Playgrounds are a strange and only partly charted territory in which are acted out status games of substantial significance for the players. The 'lore and language' of children's relationships with one another outside the classroom have not figured largely in educational discussion; yet I remember break and lunchtimes as the most important part of my schooldays, looked forward to, feared and relished at the same time. The primary playground is richer from a folklore point of view, but learning in the grubby, adolescent world at the back of the gymnasium should not be underestimated. It is here that children learn what human nature is; their History lessons may be motiveless cavalcades, but Machiavelli is present every day in the grounds. Gambling syndicates, masturbation circles, bullying, smoking, seasonal crazes (elastic bands, matchboxes, conkers, fireworks, squeezy bottles), fights and a host of other unofficial activities are the occasion for learning the sense that is developed hardly at all by writing essays or juggling numbers. The comprehensive playground is a unique social community that does not and cannot exist anywhere else.

In the divided and stratified housing estates and the infinite fragments of work, people are insulated against a perception of their own society. They eat apart, work apart and sleep apart, in intimate contact with small numbers of their peers. Stand and terrace, tennis club and bingo: mass society allows few glimpses of itself, but at school large numbers of people meet on terms of unparalleled equality. Children gravitate nevertheless towards others with whom they share similarities and connections. Secondary-age pupils already have a well-developed sense of self; they know how other children react to them and know their own instinctive status in the different hierarchies of classroom, playground and sports field. Neighbourhoods are not monoliths but varied mosaics reflected in all their richness by school. The common school draws together these diverse groups and makes them part of a whole in a remarkable social experiment. A passing visitor would be unable to distinguish sheep from goats; and indeed, teachers themselves, armed with batteries of standardised tests and long professional experience, do not easily discern social or intellectual contours by which to divide pupils into types or categories. Some critics resort to disparaging whole neighbourhoods (e.g. the 'inner city') apparently unaware of the innumerable variations in circumstances influencing education in any location.[3]

Schools attempt to influence the natural social structure by their own banding and setting arrangements.[4] It is possible by these means to influence children's expectations and self-perception but much more difficult to engineer changes in social relations in the neighbourhood outside, particularly when the intake is drawn from several estates divided by major roads or bus travel. The curriculum, intended or unintended, can confirm or extend children's pictures of themselves in relation to educational objectives, but learning must still build upon the culture and language of the pupils' environment. Schools can show what is possible but cannot make it happen.

Clubs and societies

Too little attention has been paid to the activities organised by teachers or senior pupils that occupy an undefined territory between the apparent freedom of the playground and the formality of lessons. At lunchtime, after school and at weekends a varied programme of sport, drama, music and leisure interests is offered by staff on a voluntary basis. Pupils are encouraged to attend but need not; teachers' enthusiasm and organising ability have a direct effect upon the commitment and interest of their students. Choirs can comprise hundreds singing with vitality and enjoyment but, as in the real world, interest declines and numbers dwindle if the conductor is unpunctual or weak.

With good teachers children willingly submit themselves to a rigorous discipline to become footballers, javelin throwers, madrigal singers, chess players, canoeists or actors. The relationship between teacher and pupil is not suddenly relaxed – performing a play or directing a cast is in fact more demanding than classroom work – but it is based on another model. The teacher becomes a coach, working alongside pupils and sharing the comradeship of the enterprise with them. The pressure, competition and abstraction of a lesson are replaced by joint exploration and activity; there is no copying or memorising, only work on specific tasks leading to a product or performance clear to everyone from the beginning. Children sense a closer and more collaborative relationship. No one is turned away; the school, not the individual pupil, wins glory or defeat; solidarity and mutuality are the natural result of well-led team work.

It is too easy to dismiss extracurricular events as a minority concern and to imagine that only remarkable teachers play a part. In fact the number involved in only an average programme of athletics meetings, team games, swimming galas, concerts, carol services, dramatic productions, musicals or summer fêtes is enormous. These are by nature community activities possible only through hundreds of contributions, large and small; enjoyable only because the hall or field is crowded and the experience shared with an audience.

Teachers rarely refuse to assist a project. The number involved depends less on individual temperament or character than on the structure provided and the quality of direction for each event. Clubs and societies need to be constantly nursed, fostered and re-invented; there are always new ideas for drawing pupils into schemes and projects so that everyone has at least a chance to join in. Outside, amateur associations offer similar activities but not the same circumstances. In the comprehensive school there is a genuine community sharing a common enterprise. Children of every class and type join together under the leadership of teachers committed to their success. Pupils with unusual gifts contribute towards making a structure that enables everyone to take a part, however limited. The role of the exceptional is an enabling one. This wholeness and purpose can be approached by few other local clubs and associations. Although there are different approaches to extracurricular work, these activities are perhaps the most successful part of the comprehensive experience. They seem to be free from the artificiality and contrivance of lessons, and the task to be performed has a logic that allows no room for educational theory.

Classroom transactions

From a pupil's eye view, lessons are the least enjoyable and most quickly forgotten element of school life. The organised, formal curriculum is designed to create a long-term product (e.g. a mathematician or an historian) with which most pupils cannot identify and which they do not really understand. Where is this catalogue of Royal families or parliamentary legislation leading? they may ask themselves. What can I do at the end of it that I could not do before? When will I need those simultaneous equations? What will I have to show for it all? This formal learning content does not relate to what they are doing or what they are likely to do; the prime fault of liberal education as derived from the grammar school is to seem as if it were an end in itself. For the children of manual workers who themselves expect to become manual workers many lessons can seem pointless. A gas fitter, bus driver, shop assistant or typist does not *need* what is offered in any vocational sense and has no motive for enjoying such material for its own sake. From the beginning of the lesson a teacher is struggling against a natural indifference that can be overcome only by exceptional efforts. The method of many classrooms (copying from books or blackboard, filling in sheets, answering closed questions) confirms rather than overcomes the children's feeling that they are on an express train through a foreign landscape they will never know.

Secondary specialists tend to be preoccupied with one or two subjects and fail to visualise the full impact of the curriculum. Imagine, for example, a day in the school life of an eleven- or twelve-year-old fresh from junior 'topics'. The morning begins with French conversation. You cannot say anything in English but you know no French. Words whizz past like squash balls and your racquet will barely move. Then Music and a little composition. What are these notes and letters? Please God, let her not ask me to sing alone. After break, Mathematics; a line written down in numbers? Like map references in Geography; if only I'd got the hang of that. But what, oh what, is a cube root? He's explaining. Just a minute, say that again. Sir! Sir! Too late, perhaps it's in the book. Next, History. Neolithic artefacts . . . don't panic, she's writing it on the board. Thank goodness. In the afternoon a varied and balanced programme comes to swimming. Clothes off, into the shower, that's it, now jump! Exhausted, slightly green, hair soaking and it's time for my best lesson. Poems about dinosaurs. What rhymes with reptile? Don't

worry too much about metre, just let the language flow.
Metre?

Every lesson has its own code or private language demanding high levels of concentration and attention. Only
those with a home support structure and the opportunity to
work alone have much chance of learning anything of con-
secutive, developing value. The rest clutch at fragments of
meaning for want of the preliminary language and concepts
with which to interpret such complex messages. Students able
to read well can be deflected from understanding by the
structure of organised learning with its tests and examinations.
History, for example, demands a skill at paraphrasing and
dissecting text books that has little to do with the subject but a
great deal to do with the approved mode of assessment.
Lessons are about individuals under pressure, with a constant
flow of exercises, assignments, tests and questions designed
to isolate students from their colleagues and the chance to
research.

The fear of being wrong, appearing foolish or otherwise
being shown up is inimical to anything recognisable as enjoying scholarship. Classes are so arranged that the natural,
inhibiting self-criticism of a teenager is increased rather than
diminished. Young people become less willing to try new
things and have the feeling that unless they can excel at an
activity it is barely worth trying. Youngsters not in set one or
two, for example, assume that they are 'hopeless' at the subject
thus classified. If they do not make the first XI squad, they
drop the sport. Both students and teachers in effect take their
cue from a theoretical distribution curve rather than from the
enjoyment or value of performance: a pupil observes the
hierarchy of merit implied by ability grouping and comes to
associate books and learning with status rather than with
understanding or pleasure.

Surprisingly, despite all the discouragement and strange-
ness of the teaching system, children work conscientiously
and with determination. Most students know that their job
prospects are only vaguely linked with examination results but
the Certificate of Secondary Education (CSE) files of even
relatively poor candidates offer impressive evidence of systematic, organised effort. Often pupils have jobs before the

results are published; many realise that a CSE grade 3–5 is but a marginal factor in their eligibility for unskilled work. Those in better sets have the motivation of competition and fear added to what might otherwise be a purer pleasure. Pupils' willingness to work hard in the face of puzzlement and institutionalised pressure is a clue to their state of mind. Despite everything they are anxious to conform, to please their parents and teachers and to satisfy themselves, as a matter of pride, that they have done their best. Skin-headed rebels are not representative heroes of an alienated but inarticulate mass. They are, rather, self-consciously delinquent and deviant, frightening their erstwhile peers as much as the authority they summon into being.

Although many pupils experience lessons in the mainly negative terms outlined above, there is a danger of accepting a half-truth as a whole one. Lessons are, for average children, often difficult and boring. And yet the children like their teachers and remember them with affection for ever. When asked whether they like school, a class will smile knowingly, implying that they have much better things to do with their time. After a holiday, or questioned privately, the response is quite different. Reluctantly pupils admit that *their* school is a good one and that they like it.

The polite, passive cooperation of pupils despite the oppressive deficiencies of their lessons has helped an unsatisfactory and discredited method to survive. Schools Council projects or enquiries[5] have regularly criticised the teacher-to-class lesson, 'chalk and talk', as over-didactic and inefficient. Teacher-centred approaches have been consistently rejected by informed educational opinion. Some bold schools have attempted alternatives; introducing experiments with individualised methods, worksheets, practical circuses, child-centred discovery learning – anything to avoid teachers teaching. Meanwhile, in most classrooms, sometimes with a guilty look over their shoulders, teachers are busily teaching, explaining, discoursing and otherwise elaborating their points, chalk in hand. At in-service centres it is no longer fashionable for the prophets of new methods to lecture; instead there are 'inputs', 'seminars' or 'workshops', but direct teaching will not go away.

The persistence of didactic methods arises in part from limited resources and large classes. There is an elementary survival strategy at work. If teachers taught fewer children and had more time for marking and preparation, lessons would be greatly altered and probably improved. Some secondary teachers, notably in RE, Drama and Music, see an unfairly large number of pupils, up to as many as 500 individuals in a week. This pressure leads to devices designed to minimise the strain. Problems of control and management are eased if each child is sitting down and listening. It is doubtful, however, whether this is sufficient to explain the form of a 'standard' lesson or its ambivalent reception by the pupils. Teachers behave like other 'crafts' practitioners and under stress fall back on techniques observed and mastered during a long apprenticeship. Pupils and teachers are equally accustomed to a repeating cycle of movements. The lecturer–actor–martinet combination is a relatively natural, logical outcome of the assumptions most teachers make. There is a syllabus to be taught; a body of knowledge to be communicated. How can this be efficiently presented to a large number of young people? The talk followed by questions followed by writing sequence is an automatic reflex; other methods seem to defy gravity.

When teachers recognise as a matter of experience that large quantities of factual information do not make for attentive or interested pupils they resort to the arts of the entertainer, bouncing with enthusiasm and quick-fire humour. Traditional methods leave teachers with little alternative but to embody their subject in their own personality, becoming Mathematics or French for the pupils. While professional expectations and external pressures prompt staff towards the verbal instruction of the young it is unrealistic to expect other methods to be readily adopted. There is no convincing rationale for such experiments except an optimistic faith in the ability of pupils to discover things for themselves. Few would attempt to organise clubs and societies on the principle of a typical lesson, nevertheless. Pupils want to act, play football or collect stamps; they do not want lectures, worksheets, facts or exposition. Active involvement is natural for all extracurricular work; as soon as the same teacher and pupils enter a

timetabled lesson, relationships are altered. Teacher-talk pre-
dominates and the instruction model seems inescapable. The
sense of facts to be learned and of ground to be covered
destroys many other possibilities and leads teachers to disregard the needs of their pupils.

There is an urgent need to review the tradition and educational theory that lead to this depressing classroom methodology. Pupils nevertheless remember, and will remember,
teachers, not lessons or even activities. They learn swiftly how
to earn approval or avoid disapproval; they are puzzled by
neutrality and amused by idiosyncrasy. Personality is of key
importance in stimulating learning, but without an appropriate method it will fail to achieve its purpose. However
teaching is organised, the interaction between personality and
method will remain fundamental to classroom transactions.
M. W. Keatinge long ago recognised the danger of placing too
much confidence in teachers with lively personalities but
appreciated at the same time that the right method is useless in
the wrong hands:

> [Some] maintain that the teacher is of more value than the
> method, and the personality than the manner of teaching. The
> personality that admits of this contrast may be little more than
> characteristics of manner or the freshness and breeziness of
> youth, excellent qualities, no doubt, but not to be counted on
> as a possession for life, while the method that admits of this
> contrast can be little more than a lifeless mechanism, a dull
> arrangement or rearrangement of subject-matter. True
> personality involves elements of self-control, while true
> method involves that control of subject-matter which in-
> creases its meaning by giving it a new form. This control of
> ideas is not found without personality, and such a personality is
> not found without the control which renders method possible;
> it is, indeed, increased by the constant effort to manipulate and
> present ideas so that the meaning which they convey shall be
> convincing and suggestive.[6]

A classroom with all its space consumed by desks and
chairs is a theatre that a teacher must stake out, creating order
and structure from territory, movement and words. Relationships have to be established by broad brushstrokes while
attitudes and individual points of contact have to be suggested

by changes of tone, asides and a species of commentary. A teacher plays the part he or she chooses but cannot help but be larger than life, dictating the terms of the transactions that take place. Success depends on the number and quality of the contacts and connections built up early in the year. If 'bonding' is once established it provides the framework within which children seek to please the teacher, relate to one another and apply themselves to the task. Where the teacher fails to establish these terms and conditions the pupils supply their own, and static electricity can be discharged in any direction.

The teacher's act is remembered long after the content of the lesson is forgotten; the process of learning remains when its substance has vanished. What pupils like and love is the exchange of the classroom, the relationships established and the orderliness and meaning that can emerge from them. Children hate disorder and indiscipline even more than their teachers do. Their most regretful utterance is: 'He couldn't control us.' Relationships must be pressed into a form before the pupils can respond to and participate in the work that a teacher guides. Thirty children packed into a room will not spontaneously plunge into knowledge and research; the subject must be mediated by a teacher and converted into an experience to which they can relate.

Pastoral care

Most schools have arranged for their pupils some form of care and guidance in addition to subject teaching. Boarding houses provide a classical model for tutorial relationships in which a single master or mistress accepts overall responsibility for a child's development. When pupils see their parents every day a system of surrogate fatherhood based on eating and sleeping arrangements is scarcely appropriate. 'Houses' depending on sporting rivalry, prefects, and shields for work and conduct have failed to recreate in state-maintained schools a sufficiently convincing imitation of Rugby or Harrow. The idea of a benevolent tutor advising and helping young people has persisted nevertheless. Teachers, whether in village, grammar or elementary schools, have been interested in welfare and happiness as well as in tests, notes and facts.

Comprehensives have extended tutorial business to solve some of the complex administrative problems arising mainly from size and diversity. Tutors liaise with up to a dozen colleagues who may teach a pupil during a week; compile reports; meet parents; advise on choices and options; monitor attendance; organise pupil lists; maintain records; conduct assemblies; plan visits, competitions and special events. Pupils, and often their parents are unaware of organisational matters, but skilful management is needed to sustain apparently routine lessons. Large schools need to involve a considerable number of tutors to ensure that children follow a continuous and effective programme of study. It is not a coincidence that comprehensives have been driven to change from 'houses' to 'years'. The focus of pastoral care is now the calendar of events that must be organised for each year group of children rather than the house that brought all ages together for mainly sporting and social activities.

Peter Dawson, in *Making a Comprehensive Work,*[7] suggests that the development of pastoral care is the distinctive contribution and achievement of the common school. The year tutor as 'middle manager' is perhaps an original contribution, but only to the solution of difficulties caused by the larger comprehensives themselves. Although a complex structure might collapse without organised pastoral care, it is doubtful whether this administrative activity in itself represents an advance on the interest and kindness shown by teachers in other types of school. Year tutors have too many clients and too little time to sustain friendly, personal contact with every student. For a majority of quiet, unobtrusive, cooperative young people in comprehensives the efficient administration of records and choices has all but replaced the tutorial relationship familiar in boarding establishments. In a day school there is little alternative to working with groups; pupils are best known, helped and supported through positive, activity-based relations with their peers and teachers. Interesting and enjoyable lessons can be the best form of care.

Advocates of a 'pastoral' approach are sometimes more ambitious than this, proposing a counselling model of 'cases' and 'treatment' derived from social work. All-ability schools include a wide range of social problems and there is an understandable temptation to offer therapy of some kind to youngsters afflicted by personal problems or psychological disturbance. Everyone suffers if problems are neglected and unsympathetic teaching can aggravate the plight of unhappy children, perhaps causing avoidable outbursts of misbe-haviour. School can be a source of security, stability and friendship in otherwise bleak, troubled young lives. Unfortu-nately there is insufficient time to provide direct personal help for more than a small number of pupils, and without adequate training teacher-counsellors can do more harm than good.

Excessive criticism has made it difficult to judge dispassion-ately the success of the comprehensive experience. Every ill of society is attributed to secondary education and teachers seem guilty by association with adolescence. After twenty-five years, however, a very large number of schools have become a focus for the aspirations of their neighbourhoods, unique communities bringing together children of all backgrounds in an extraordinary and creative range of activities. By compari-son with their restricted and divisive predecessors comprehen-sives have an excellent record.

It is not enough. Few princes and princesses have emerged from comprehensive gates. Teachers have taken the 'ordinary man' from the shadows of history (and of 'his betters'), but there is still a grave danger that he may be blinded and run away. Comprehensive schools have not escaped the self-help, self-improvement ethos of the tripartite system and a distinc-tive method and content has not been established. Too much that happens in the classroom is watered down or handed down, rooted in false ideas about children and learning, apparently pessimistic about their future. A rescue is not feasible until a more comprehensive view of talent and learn-ing is widely accepted as a basis for new methods of teaching.

CHAPTER 2

Theories of learning

Consider the case of a basketball coach at the start of a new year, with a group of healthy eleven-year-olds. He does not medically examine the boys to discover their strength or degree of physical coordination. He does not have a set of notes or deliver a lecture on the principles of invasion games or the history of Afro-American sportsmen. Pupils are not expected to learn the rules of basketball or practise by themselves. Instead the coach takes his players to the gymnasium, pointing out its main features and reminding everyone about suitable kit. Children are in small mixed-ability groups to ensure that no team has an unfair advantage in practice or competition. As more effective shooters or dribblers emerge they are distributed evenly. The coach directs a constant flow of activities, explaining each step to be learned before giving the youngsters a chance to try it for themselves. He passes amongst the squad suggesting improvements in technique, drawing attention to good models. Each skill is practised in short bursts, routines with an element of competition and fun. Drills build upon one another: shooting, dribbling, passing, movements, angles.

There is a cumulative effect as each aspect is developed and integrated with other features of the game. Players continually perform the movements involved in learning basketball; pace and variety are part of a natural sequence. Children work in teams, developing an understanding of one another as well as efficiency in all dimensions of physical activity; coordinating hand and eye, maintaining fitness, developing spatial awareness and anticipating the moves and stratagems of others. There is no end-of-term examination or individual testing, although several highly competitive, hard-fought contests will have taken place. Some pupils will be better players than others but everyone will have played a great deal of the sport. The amount each pupil learns is not related to initial or natural ability; teaching and interest are crucial. The school or county naturally selects the most outstanding players for league competition but this is an extra and does not affect what happens in lessons.

In mainstream classroom subjects like English or Mathematics teachers seldom adopt such an apparently obvious and sensible approach. They seem to be preoccupied with discriminating between individual children and devising lessons according to set formulae for varying levels of presumed learning ability. Active, group-work methods seem to be prevented by a formal, 'academic' attitude to subject content and assessment criteria. Teachers, under the influence of professional and subject traditions, appear to select unnatural and psychologically unsound coaching schemes. It is important to understand the theory of learning that leads to these results, and to suggest an alternative.

Intelligence and ability

Sir Cyril Burt's ideas about intellectual development, applied and popularised as a result of his work for the LCC, helped to establish the notion of intelligence as an inherited, intrinsic ability upon which learning depends. Many local authorities, following London's lead, used intelligence tests to select individual children for an education appropriate for their 'type' of ability. The civil service and other public and private enterprises have since made use of IQ (intelligence quotient) tests to assess aptitude and suitability for positions within their ranks.

The system of education adopted after the Butler Education Act in 1944 depended on the validity and reliability of such tests to select pupils for grammar, technical or modern schools.

Burt's main point was that individuals learn and develop without external stimulus or social contact. As children's innate potential for learning unfolds they are supposed to acquire a knowledge of objects and movement, and to develop skills in their manipulation and use. Learning is perceived as an abstract, cerebral activity, through which the world of sense data is processed and classified. Understanding is described as an agglomeration of empirical, measurable processes. Culture, family and friends are peripheral to automatic intellectual growth. Children do not learn more effectively as a result of practice or experience; 'intelligence' cannot be taught. Pupils are presumed to have certain fixed ceilings of attainment that can be related to age and measured accordingly. The performance of individuals is compared with norms based upon the results of many tests so that the tests themselves define the maxima and minima of performance. Students are differentiated according to their ability level or type. Some never achieve full human thought, while others are especially gifted. Children's thinking differs from adults' because intelligence develops sequentially. The same intelligence factor is assumed to apply to most activities.

Modern investigators, in the main, have tried to extend IQ tests to improve their validity, not to look at learning from other points of view. Writers like Liam Hudson[1] or Edward de Bono (whose phrase 'lateral thinking' has almost entered the popular vocabulary) have added new dimensions like 'creativity' or 'divergence' without changing the main idea of cognitive ability as an individual, inherited, innate potential. The most recent research suggests as many as seven dimensions of intelligence, including social and personal qualities in addition to the traditional categories of verbal and numerical reasoning. Many still think of 'intelligence' as a general 'brightness' (or 'dimness') measurable on a graduated scale and unaltered by environment. According to their scores on pencil-and-paper tests children can be pinned upon a normal distribution curve like a donkey's tail.

IQ represents a prediction about maximum future performance, not a reflection of attainment. It can be inferred from test results that some groups of pupils will prove incapable of certain mental operations. There is thought to be no need to explain high achievement or poor performance because these are biological in origin, a congenital feature of a fixed proportion of the population. Potential may be unfulfilled through lack of effort but each student has a discoverable, limited ability.

The main influence of the intelligence idea was exerted through scholarship and eleven-plus examinations. Pupils with high scores were chosen for an education derived from the public schools and classically described as 'academic'. This has established a firm and mutually reinforcing connection in teachers' minds between two doubtful propositions. 'Intelligent' pupils were selected for an 'academic' education. The public and grammar schools offered a model of secondary education broadly linguistic and liberal in character; it was designed for pupils aiming at public service examinations or the universities. People good at IQ tests were selected for this high status tradition without further enquiry into the nature of the intelligence or the 'academic' matter to which it was to be applied. The term 'academic' was soon used to designate gifted pupils, implying a capacity for abstraction and theory, for higher level thinking. The study of books and languages came to seem abstract and theoretical, suitable activities for highly 'intelligent' pupils with an innate superiority in thinking. This intellectual élite, recruited without social prejudice, would not be expected to learn in the sense of the basketball example. They would, rather, be fed facts and ideas that their brains would absorb automatically.

After 1944 pupils not chosen for an 'academic' education were sent to secondary moderns where the curriculum was based upon the only readily available and sufficiently economical model, the elementary or board school. It was believed that less 'intelligent' pupils, deficient in reasoning, would have more aptitude for useful, practical skills, a fact that coincided with their presumed employment destinations. To the curriculum theorists of those days, practical activity did not seem to require a capacity for abstract thought; the coordination of hand and eye was considered a lower order skill. Pupils not qualifying for grammar schools were thus associated with practical work and manual employment.

This history is responsible for a short-hand that divides pupils into two sets, 'intelligent' or 'less intelligent' ('able' or 'less able'), and education into two parallel stereotypes, 'academic' and 'practical'. The range of ability described by Burt's intelligence curve has in practice been startlingly compressed so that only two broad categories of student were recognised by the tripartite system. Questions of degree were eliminated; children were clever or not. The cut-off point for merit was not explained. Teachers came to think of children as 'academic' or 'non-academic' and when selection ceased the classification continued. Children were visualised or described as if learning were one-dimensional like height, either 'academic' or 'practical', 'bright' or 'dim', 'able' or 'less able'. Questions like 'in relation to what?' or 'in what circumstances?' were not put. The notion of children either possessing or not possessing ability, derived from intelligence tests and eleven-plus selection, has persisted in comprehensive schools.

A highly simplified, two-tier profile of talent, dividing pupils into natural groups, has been used to distinguish 'O' level and CSE candidates, to identify able Mathematicians and Linguists (for extension studies, perhaps in Additional Maths or a second language) and to justify setting and banding arrangements. Banding relies on the assumption that pupils 'able' at French are also good at Mathematics and English, or some similar group of subjects. Banding or streaming is common in most secondary schools after the first year and reflects the application of this simplified working model of ability by many Heads and teachers.

Comprehensive schools continue to rely upon a view of learning based on levels of inherited ability, despite doubts about intelligence testing and selection. Few study children as the basketball coach must to discover their diverse talents. Instead there is an empty tautology. If a pupil learns effectively he or she is defined as 'bright'; their success at learning is then ascribed to an innate potentiality.

The limits of intelligence

The suggestion that apparently different processes of learning and activity stem from a single, inherited factor that teachers cannot much influence has been under sustained attack for some years.[2] Researchers working in this field today would be embarrassed by some of the educational consequences of past intelligence testing and would wish to enter sophisticated qualifications to many of the points sketched above. Burt himself has been discredited and it seems as though he invented his own evidence. Although the complexity of human thought is now more fully recognised, the working hypothesis that children are bright or dim, academic or practical, remains to discourage deeper enquiry about the nature of learning. Crude versions of the intelligence theory have led some teachers to accept low achievement as an almost natural phenomenon, a reflection of a lack of ability rather than a cultural product compounded by inappropriate methods. Children, rather than teaching methods, have been blamed for their own lack of success.

The strong correlations observed between measures of school attainment and indices of home background suggest that social and economic factors exert a powerful influence on pupil performance. Any account of learning that does not explain how poverty or low status might cause children to fail at school must be unsatisfactory. Sir Cyril solved the problem with the circular, Social Darwinist argument that low intelligence made people poor so that no one should expect intellectual achievement in a deprived area. This is no longer convincing because testers now recognise that the effects of culture or experience cannot be excluded from testing. IQ questions include a selection of puzzles and codes in an attempt to bypass content but rarely avoid referring to taught concepts or facts. Numerical reasoning, for example, can appear to be neutral, a pure form of intelligence. A child with a grounding in the principles of New Mathematics, however, would surely have some advantage over another whose introduction to arithmetic was marked by incompetent and unsympathetic teaching or rote learning methods.

It is easier to agree upon an innate base for number ability than it is to accept that progress is independent of the teacher or the content and methods employed. Verbal reasoning tests are still more vulnerable to this criticism. The use of sequences and codes involving missing words or letters may cloud the distinction between Algebra and Shakespeare but they do not prove that language develops independently from experience. It is at least possible that attitudes and relationships impinge on the learning process so early that the most abstract-seeming items cannot be guaranteed to exclude their effects. Cultural factors can exert the most subtle influence.

Intelligence tests that turn out to measure only previous experience, or the understanding of particular concepts, will have no more general significance or predictive value than any other assessment item.[3] The usefulness of IQ tests would then be restricted. A result on a batch of questions related to numerical reasoning, for example, may give acceptable guidance about future performance in Arithmetic or Mathematics, but not in Art or History. General conclusions drawn from single tests are unlikely to be well founded. The design of specific tests to measure particular aspects or dimensions of intelligence to improve the validity of IQ can also produce a misleadingly mechanical picture of children's thinking. As each element is described, from the cognitive to the affective, an image is suggested of interconnecting levers clicking into position, areas of the brain responding in logical order to external cues. Increasingly varied and elaborate batteries of tests have been constructed covering innumerable aspects of performance, each of which is supposed to have a distinct existence. This is the utilitarian tradition in which even happiness is explained in terms of sense data received! Regularities or patterns in scores on component items of IQ tests are interpreted as evidence for the existence of psychological properties that can be examined separately through ingenious puzzles. Their operation is supposed to be predictable, and together they represent general intelligence.

Although this scheme reflects the efforts of testers to reduce the intangible workings of children's minds to measurable proportions, it is no easy matter to maintain the boundaries of each category or 'bundle' of skills. Scores are open to indefinite reinterpretation because philosophical as well as technical issues are raised by defining thought so that it can be measured. What is meant, for example, by 'observation'? Is it a question of eyesight or memory? Can you observe without understanding? Can you deduce or imagine without having observed? Each successive word or phrase used to subdivide human thought for tests or to qualify what is meant by 'creative' or 'imaginative'[4] entails a fresh difficulty. Verbal or spatial reasoning, creativity or observation almost belong to the phrenological world of wisdom and benevolence. Skills merge into one another as attempts at definition are made and a composite 'general intelligence' seems less and less convincing.

The preponderance of reasoning and calculating items in intelligence tests has contributed to this mechanistic image. The need to test and measure uncontaminated ability inevitably results in abstraction with mental activity portrayed as computer-like. Code-breaking, Rubic cube solving, calculating and analysing by logical steps are, for this reason, given a false priority. The aesthetic, goal-setting element of thought is understated and emphasis is given to data-processing 'inputs' and 'outputs'. The balance is not readily restored by introducing a test of aesthetic perception or empathy because these qualities are not self-contained elements but part of the warp and weft of all mental processes. The picture of learning as an exercise of innate skills, which have to be tested singly and in the abstract to establish their existence, is unhelpful to teachers. If the possibility is admitted that events and experiences might simultaneously engage every aspect of a child's being, so that no one can readily distinguish emotion from reason or intuition from deduction, these categories become even more clouded.

The danger of approaching teaching with this type of hypothesis is that divisions like that between 'academic' and 'practical' learning discussed above may seem logical and scientific rather than artificial. In reality, hand, eye and brain work together; artists are as theoretical and practical as scientists. Who can say what it is that leads one human being to observe and interpret objects through light and colour and another to consider the physics of heavenly bodies? Theory and practice[5] are naturally inseparable and yet a theory of

innate ability prior to and unaffected by experience encourages
just such a dualist distinction.

A perhaps more harmful consequence of the idea of inherited intelligence is the encouragement it gives teachers to think
of children's ability as governed by fixed limits and norms.
The benchmark for measuring any work by pupils is provided
by a distribution curve, not by an appreciation of its intrinsic
worth. A good performance is, by definition, one that is above
average; everything else represents a form of failure. Too
much should not be expected; improvement is possible only
up to a point. By these means a majority of children are found
wanting, limited by their genetic endowment and unable to
perform at an adequate level on essential tasks. Ordinary
people, whatever the circumstances of school and culture, are
considered incapable of 'higher level' thinking. In fact IQ tests
say nothing about the *content* or *value* of a particular performance; their contribution is to arrange marks in an age-related
rank order. What a score of 140 means in relation to present or
future work is still a matter of human judgement, for all the
semi-scientific apparatus of testing.

This is not to discount a genetic foundation for mental
operations or to deny that there is an inherited starting point
for learning. What is unacceptable, however, is the suggestion
that these initial differences are of permanent importance,
setting definite ceilings to achievement. It has been shown that
teaching, experience and culture contribute to what people can
do. The case for regarding some pupils as congenitally incapable of certain types of activity is a poor one. Hereditary
influences can be acknowledged without teachers being disabled. There are, for example, more factors influencing the
development of basketball players than inherited size, power
and health. From an early age, diet, training, encouragement,
family interest, opportunity, personal inclination and peer
group pressures will have preconditioned youngsters who, at
age eleven, appear to differ only in natural endowment. Some
elements are more important than others. Fatty foods, alcohol
or smoking can ruin the young athlete; a sympathetic and
skilful coach can open possibilities otherwise closed. Trans-
port and facilities may be decisive. Character can contribute as
much to success as natural gifts.

Eugenic notions predispose comprehensive teachers to adopt a meritocratic perception of the evidence of their eyes. Many still look at children from a selective point of view, and public examinations propel schools in a similar direction. The fact that some children perform better than others has become more important than the pleasure and personal enrichment everyone can obtain from mental or physical exertion. And yet the basketball example illustrates what is possible. Some players dribble and shoot with great aplomb but this is not allowed to overshadow the perfectly acceptable efforts of everyone else. Ordinary healthy children can run, leap and jump when the lesson is like a session in the gymnasium. What is required is a system of coaching, facilities and organisation designed to foster active participation for all. Basketball provides a suggestive parallel for those interested in intellectual development. In the absence of age or illness people can perform for themselves all the physical tasks and activities necessary for effective living, from driving and walking to cooking and sewing. Is it not likely that the same is true of mental operations, that the majority of the population is perfectly capable of learning and thinking at a level adequate to meet the demands of life in a self-governing community?

Intelligence tests raise questions and difficulties far more numerous than those they resolve. Their validity depends on excluding precisely the cultural effects and educational content with which teachers are most concerned. Their assumptions and hypotheses rest upon doubtful scientific foundations. An alternative view of learning is needed to provide the rationale for a new curriculum and new methods of teaching. Without a distinct and comprehensive theory of talent most children will continue to be taught according to traditions that have their origins in selective education, whatever reforms are proposed or introduced.

'Darren': portrait of a pupil[6]

A rather large, scruffy fourteen-year-old lad lolls at a classroom desk. There is some hair on his sallow face and a half-smirk plays on his lips as he turns his head towards his neighbour. If he is asked a direct question he is flummoxed and embarrassed; enthusiasm is not his stock-in-trade. Nor is neat handwriting, as the tattered exercise book on the table shows. It contains some ill-written, disjointed prose punctuated by diagrams drawn without a ruler. On the cover is the legend 'Skins rule o.k.' The boy is reluctant to study and sees homework and lessons as intrusions on liberty. Unsupervised, he sneaks a cigarette with his friends. He is not a typical pupil but is a familiar enough habitué of the modern school. To penetrate the mystery of under-achievement it is necessary to understand Darren's mode of learning.

IQ and reading-age tests provide some narrowly focused information suggesting that he is below average, one of the majority who do neither well nor badly, part of the central arc of the distribution curve. His essays are as short as he thinks the teacher will accept and score either 6 or 7 out of 10. His reports reflect the extent to which he has cooperated with various projects and a vague sense of his competence and personality. His year tutor can add comments on his cheerfulness, participation in activities and attitude towards school life. He could 'do better if he tried harder'; he has 'the ability but does not always use it'. This modern, mass-production student is not 'bright' but no one is quite sure if he is less able; there are many others as remote from the 'standards' of GCE culture. Darren's teachers comment upon him intuitively, fastening on impressions of capability or character and most aware of the fact that he does not write well enough to succeed at school. He is the kind of student of whom very little is expected; whatever the subject the salient remarks are the same. Darren 'does not concentrate', 'does not work hard enough' or 'does not apply himself'. Teachers identify these general attitudinal factors as critical for school achievement; few remarks are made about the particular skills required for different areas of the curriculum. It is rare for a History teacher to suggest how a pupil might empathise more effectively or develop powers of analysis or imagination; scientists seldom indicate how skills may be improved or hypotheses formed. None of Darren's exercises seem designed to develop or improve specific skills and none are assessed to highlight strengths or shortcomings of this nature.

A misleading, unfavourable impression can emerge from observing Darren's behaviour in the artificial and pressurised atmosphere of the classroom. From his dour and unresponsive manner broad conclusions are drawn. Schools expect enthusiasm and hard work, yet even high-flying university students may succumb to peer group pressure, taking pains to conceal their interest, at times finding study less attractive than drink. A pupil who speaks coherently in class is bound to seem 'too clever by half' to his peers; one teacher can scarcely hope for a natural, controlled dialogue with thirty children. Many of Darren's most unhappy characteristics reflect adolescence rather more than the curriculum, and his parents and teachers mourn the loss of his childhood in their comments on his present performance. Sometimes he is subjected to biting sarcasm as he stumbles after the answer with bovine goodwill. Positive qualities can be entirely lost. In the playground he may be a leader of men, or at least prove himself equipped for survival on the streets or in the black economy of the unemployed young.

Darren's facility with racing odds and darts scores is beside the point in Mathematics; his smart and helpful appearance when serving at the tool shop on Saturday would puzzle those staff who battle with his T-shirt during the week. His friends find him calm and sensible, a reliable friend; after work-experience, an employer reports similar qualities. It is not, however, until his personal history is unravelled that a more profound or sympathetic understanding of his ability is possible and an explanation can be given of his lack of success in approved activities.

Early learning and child development

From birth Darren's life and learning are indistinguishable from one another, a muddled liaison governed by serendipity as much as by any biological law. Physical, emotional and intellectual development blend together in an irregular, uneven pattern, jolted by events, discoveries and fear. The boy's whole body and personality is engaged and absorbed by life, which is shaped by waves of sensation and emotion stemming from human relationships. His parents may be warm or tense, anxious or reassuring, detached or encompassing, but each move of theirs prompts a response in him. Each feeling they evoke is related to an increasingly differentiated array of symbols, sensations, sounds, lights, colours, appetites and textures.

In his early days, sounds and smiles are perhaps the most important, the essential elements of a baby's communication system. Initially, smiling, babbling and listening are spontaneous, depending on physical development. They become learned behaviour, practised in a continuing flow of cues and responses. No child has the same experience or gives the same signals. Sucking, cuddling, crying, bathing, changing and playing provide endless opportunities for learning and experimenting, for the creation of an intimate but sophisticated parent–child dialogue.

Darren's infant contribution is close to that of an adult, often more complex than mothers at first recognise. E. M. Forster's phrase[7] 'only connect' hints at how children and grown-ups link and associate images, building structures that help predict what will happen next. Babies crying can be as subtle as Renaissance diplomats – they have no stiletto or secret code for correspondence but their apprentice manipulation is often as cunning as any adult display of temper or tantrum. What is described as thinking in the empirical, rational version often is no more than a lightning shaft through layers of experience, a sudden movement of a spider across a network of remembrance. Reason and logic are more in evidence after the thought than before it, justifying the dash across silken strands in the end unable to bear the weight placed upon them.

Learning depends upon human relationships. The greater part of education is therefore social in character. Most knowledge, especially that understood by children, is of people and how they behave, not of things and their mechanisms. What Darren knows before his fifth year is how to relate to people. Extending outwards from his mother to his father, siblings, relatives and neighbours, the infant grows in his mastery of communication systems and their associated emotional and cultural charge. His success in this early learning has been shown to depend on a secure attachment and a sustained sense of security. The disruption of relationships – whether by rows, grief, separation or rejection – can be observed to destroy concentration and logic even in quite mature and previously stable individuals.

Early experiences of people, potties, sex and food, rated so highly by Freud and so low by Burt, cannot be sensibly distinguished from other modes of learning. Smiling, sucking, talking, writing, dancing, composing and Mathematics belong to the same continuum. What is learned, however, is not fixed or tangible, a piece of jigsaw pressed into a permanent, definite position. Each new experience or impression is, rather, a flavour added to an existing mixture, a charged molecule that changes what it joins yet is absorbed or even overwhelmed by the sediment at the bottom of the flask. Trauma, stress, success, rewards and punishments are part of what is learned and help shape future responses. Memory is heavily influenced by emotional events so that selective forgetfulness helps to change what is taken in. Some learning, especially that relating to often-repeated actions or physical manipulation (e.g. number tables, driving, bouncing a ball), becomes autonomous and tends to relate to functional efficiency. The results of more subjective experiences are less easily calculated. Everything that happens is viewed through a personal prism of previous history: Darren's response and subsequent recollection will be his own. The constant effort of tests and examinations to ensure that pupils learn the same concepts/facts from the same lessons seems futile in this light.

This view of learning contrasts sharply with the 'academic'/'practical' schema adopted by many teachers. It is focused upon people and how they communicate with one another. Everyone, from an early age, responds to events as a developing human soul, susceptible to influence and change. Some may be more adept than others but each carries the permanent mark of previous successful or unsuccessful experiments. All are human, whatever the inherited limits of muscle and nerve, and have a potential to come to terms with the demands of life. Although essentially speculative, this account is based on the ideas of optimistic, anti-determinist psychologists and their recent researches into child development.[8]

Without such a conception it would be difficult indeed to account for personality.

How do politics, religion and other values come to run in families and neighbourhoods? How else can the transmission of culture, class or ethnic characteristics be explained? Is cookery learned on a native hearth so different from science mastered in a laboratory? Is 'thinking ability' likely to be divorced from other aspects of human psychology?

These ideas help explain the contrast between Darren's rich experience of life and complex potential for response, on one hand, and his poor classroom performance, on the other. Emotional disturbance and insecurity; the attitude of parents, peers and neighbourhood; the failure of school to build on his earlier experience of learning; a gulf between the literary world of teachers and the human world of pupils; impoverished relationships in childhood; Darren's own values and interests: all these might help explain how fourteen years' engagement with life come to be discounted in the simple phrase 'less able'.

One example shows how this conception of pupils and teachers at cross-purposes can be applied to explain under-achievement. History teachers rely upon a vocabulary that is for them natural and for their pupils baffling. 'Liberalism', 'nationalism' and 'feudalism', for example, are apparently inescapable terms without which understanding of the broad movements of the past seems impossible. Recognising the difficulty, many text-books and teachers confine themselves to the most simple language, descriptive writing and story-telling. It is assumed that children's failure to make sense of 'liberalism' and similar abstractions stems from some immaturity in their reasoning. From youngsters' naive use of language and inability to manipulate phrases like 'free trade', 'political obligation', or 'representative government' is inferred an underlying lack of understanding of historical ideas. It has even been suggested that most schoolchildren are incapable of the level of thought necessary for an appreciation of the past.

It is a matter of experience, nevertheless, that nearly all children can buy and sell without being cheated, know the value of money, can subvert or exploit restrictive or indulgent parents, desire their say in decisions affecting them and know their place and its significance in the hierarchy of the school.

From infancy they have experienced freedom and authority, and can identify with Gladstone's indignation with the dungeons of King Bomba or the misery of Ireland. Children find it difficult to apply their experiences of restriction and confinement (whether economic or political) to History because abstract terms (like 'liberalism') create a premature distance between life and the study of life.

Lessons somehow maintain a gap between experience and language so that children's potential for understanding History is only partially realised. The treatment of topics in text-books seems designed to minimise interest and to avoid a bridge between pupils and the past. No attempt is made to begin with immediate relationships or to use pupils' language or experiences. Instead there is a steadfast reliance on a literary medium. Exposition and explanation are similarly couched in an abstruse language with few points of contact for an urban or suburban teenager. Questions are arranged in the format of a comprehension test, depending on a high degree of accuracy in the use of syntax and vocabulary. History teaching characteristically closes the alternative routes to understanding, reducing learning to a solitary, formal mode.[9]

Despite this discouragement some pupils do advance. Those who are used to talking at home and are accustomed to discussing events and reflecting upon them have an advantage over the others. Some pupils have been encouraged to write, to respond, to develop original trains of thought. If verbal forms of this kind are not valued at home, a pupil can hardly acquire such language *at the same time* as a set of sophisticated abstract terms commonly used only by a small number of intellectuals. If Darren is not, from an early point, refining his use of language and converting his ideas into symbolic form so much will always remain immediate, personal and local.

This example also illustrates the danger of statements about what children can and cannot do. Darren can understand all the ideas involved in his History lessons; what he cannot do is to convert his experiences into classroom terms or perceive, unaided, a connection between himself and people in the past. These insights provide a promising foundation for a revised teaching method[10] designed to develop children's existing understanding.

Language and literacy

The 'liberalism' example demonstrates that unsatisfactory work, attributed in the past to deficiencies of innate intelligence, can often be more precisely explained as a failure to communicate effectively, especially in writing. Children whose relationships and social connections are linguistically impoverished, especially when they are very young, have little opportunity to develop and integrate their experiences. Language is an intrinsic part of the web of contacts a child forms with people, their behaviour and the external world. Its content depends on imitation of available models; youngsters adopt the style, accent, intonation, grammar, vocabulary and even set phrases of their family and neighbourhood. Their babble may have a natural tendency to become speech but for content and quality is dependent on parental conversation.

There are indications that these experiences of language absorbed through social transactions are of fundamental importance, an essential enabling factor for further learning. Some pupils have a vocabulary several hundred words greater than their contemporaries on *entry* to primary school; it is an advantage in the development and use of experience for which it is hard to provide compensation. This is a natural result of the interdependence of thought and language described by Paul Hirst:

> Intelligible thought necessarily involves symbols of some sort and most of it involves the symbols of our common languages . . . concepts and propositions are units of meaning and not psychological entities, pseudo-objects or events . . . Understanding a form of thought necessarily involves mastering the use of the appropriate language game.[11]

The ceaseless early flow of communications (from smiles and caresses to food and chatter) is gradually refined into symbolic form because thought depends on representations of reality; a child cannot learn on the basis of inchoate sensation. Order and structure are essential for memory and development. Where early experiences are charged with negative emotions, or when parents do not enter into a sufficiently articulate dialogue (for whatever reason), a child is likely to fall behind in self-expression *and* understanding. Possible sources of individual differences are accentuated by social and cultural factors.

Some families and communities have marked advantages compared with others that are inevitably transferred to the children. The wealth and leisure enjoyed by some social groups has been historically converted into formal, written education, into reading and reflection. Professional, clerical and managerial occupations give greater emphasis to the elaboration and use of language while for others (particularly those casually or manually employed) words are of minimal importance for most activities. These differences are consolidated and made almost permanent as each generation reads, listens and participates in parental dialogue and local conversation. Complexities of syntax and meaning, the range of uses of language and more abstract ideas are accumulated by families over many years, generating an indefinable cultural capital.

Class and status do not necessarily coincide with richness of language and culture. There is no sense in which the chatter of golfers or the lounge bar is superior to that of a betting shop or bingo hall. Rotary lunches, cocktail parties or church fêtes have their own set patterns of talk, none of which has more sense or substance than the lively debates of miners' clubs, Methodist chapels or a shop stewards' meeting. People find the language to express their experience. A sense of injustice can be as powerful a dynamo of graphic, high quality utterance as the most mannered leisure. Local experience can be dismissed as limited and parochial provided it is recognised that every parish has a similar tendency to interpret the world from its own rather simple and self-referential propositions. The possession of a complex frame of reference, through which comparisons can be made and conflicting notions be examined and contrasted, comes from the promptings of urgent experience rather than superior intelligence or genetic advantages. Language depends less upon the gift of an individual than upon the access of a community to leisure, books and the shared, collective knowledge that can undermine customs and conventions. The voice that must be heard is one striving to reconcile discord or appease dissatisfaction, a task for which language and ideas are needed. It is, after all, the purpose of education to integrate local and familial experiences into a formal discourse that reaches beyond a single community and makes possible contrast, comparison and synthesis. An educated person does not depend upon personal, subjective experience for their knowledge or understanding. The lead some children possess indicates the power of education, not its futility. School and college have a multiplier effect as dynamic as any in economics.

The common school has within it children differentiated primarily by the degree to which local and personal commentary has given place to a fully articulate, accumulated literacy. It is an error to assume that everyone can respond at once to complex forms of writing and equally mistaken to dismiss as defective or half-human those disadvantaged by personal circumstances of family or neighbourhood.

The grand strategic error of the comprehensive school is to begin teaching with the abstract language and prose that it is the task of education to create. An effective teaching method will begin with pupils and their relationships, not with textbooks and foreign tongues. The aim must be to develop to the full the natural, local, active language all the children possess and through which they at present understand one another; to enrich and extend that form, reaching towards literacy through written exercises arising from an experience to which the child can relate in personal terms. Teachers must focus upon a shared, group communication and experience. This more natural approach to language, starting from the personal, particular and the group, and working towards the general and written, will give access points for everyone. Those enjoying a lead already will also benefit because such a plan is founded in a recognition of the social, human nature of learning and avoids the artificiality of current methods. This is more fully discussed in Chapter 5.

Merit and citizenship

Meritocratic, self-help ideas stress the importance of individuals, discounting the influence of family and culture and relying upon scientific measurements to identify those who can succeed. Their effect is to demean and diminish large numbers of pupils and to accept their misfortune, if misfortune it is, as personal and inevitable. At an unconscious level such a theory of learning leaves teachers with no alternative but to regard perhaps a majority of their pupils as less fully developed and less human, less qualified to form judgements or accept responsibility.

Children lose their dignity and much of their self-esteem if teachers think of them as in some strange sense incomplete or imperfect. The intelligence concept also diminishes thought by describing literate, humane activities in terms of abstractions and codes. The political implication of this doctrine is that specialists of merit must be found to act in the interests of those unfit to decide for themselves. The talents of ordinary people are portrayed as insufficient for the decisions implicit in citizenship or the management of public affairs.

As a theory of government this is unpersuasive. It is rare for people to solve problems as if they were desiccated calculating machines, analysing a puzzle with cold impartiality from first principles. A decision-maker is much more likely to be guided by underlying attitudes and assumptions, a compass forged by experience. Political decisions about priorities depend on value judgements that are more than random preferences or the product of abstract Mathematics. All citizens are influenced by clusters of feelings that filter and shape the material impressions or evidence with which they are presented. Logical deduction is secondary to a continuous editorial process by which new information is judged and responses are measured. This is why it is so rare for people considered intelligent to convert one another by argument.

Beliefs and values reflect a view of the world deeply entwined with the history of particular neighbourhoods and communities; they are not, in origin at least, individual. People live, inescapably, in their own time and place. They share in group experiences and absorb a species of folk wisdom that they use later to evaluate issues apparently remote from their personal frame of reference.

Attempts to describe this process of response and decision in terms of individual intelligence or supposed skills (e.g. analysis, logic, deduction) are likely to prove forlorn. Policy-making, administration and management seem increasingly similar to other aspects of learning – public activity arising from past interests and events and themselves contributing to further understanding and development. Important decisions do not often take an abstract or technical form, although advice may be given and needed. The rationalistic model underestimates the degree to which politics are about aesthetic and moral questions, about choosing whom to trust, whom to support or whose proposal is most likely to be beneficial.

Common-sense judgements of value and behaviour are therefore accessible to everyone who has grown up in human society, and are in no sense dependent on remarkable powers of abstract analysis, special knowledge or expertise. Self-government requires nothing that is not involved in the education and development of ordinary people. Everyone can attain a sufficient quality of understanding; all are worthy and fit. This does not mean that everyone will necessarily decide to participate or that there will be equality in the distribution of political effort.

If common sense and experience are the essence of learning and citizenship, as this argument suggests, it is not too late to rescue the comprehensive experience so that the ordinary person can 'wield the royal sceptre'. Until now the organisation, curriculum, teaching methods and assessment practice of the common school have been borrowed from the self-improving individualism of the grammar and public schools. Teachers have concerned themselves with exceptional pupils and excellent performances, at times despairing of a recalcitrant majority. The search for intelligence-based merit and opportunities for individual advancement has compromised the self-governing learning community that might have been. Now, disappointed at the results, some are ready to abandon schools altogether while others want to reform children and families instead, perhaps wishing to eliminate a misunderstood class culture.

This is an unhelpful and unnecessary pessimism. It would be wise to follow Jeremy Bentham in taking 'men as they are and the law as it might be'. The remaining chapters suggest a strategy for 'second generation' comprehensive schools, proposing changes that will enable children to join together in learning activities that unite rather than divide neighbourhoods and that lead naturally to a self-governing society.

CHAPTER 3

Leadership and change

Most comprehensive schools are managed and organised like a major but conventional theatrical production. The Head-teacher directs, or is expected to direct, the school as if it were a Shakespearian drama, selecting a cast of players to win a competition of some kind. All authority is vested in the director so that the stage manager, house manager, technicians, cast and even audience depend upon an oracle for their activity and entertainment. Parents choose schools because of the Head and interpret their children's education through a single leader.

It is difficult to see how this can be a satisfactory framework for developing self-government, however understood, or how pupils and teachers might be encouraged to collaborate in active learning by such methods. On the contrary, the reliance placed upon authority and hierarchy discourages everyone from taking initiatives or accepting responsibility. Schools seem to play their part in conditioning young people to accept knowledge as if it were faith and to suppress critical impulses. Teachers demand obedience and rely upon established practices; pupils are trained to believe what they are told by specialists.

The transition to a more participatory form of school

government in which relationships are organised to promote effective learning by everyone is complicated by a paradox. Change requires a positive leadership that could increase rather than reduce dependence upon a charismatic figure with a private if heroic vision of the future. It is a familiar political problem: how to use authority to create the possibility of freedom. At present schools are organised as if their purpose were to draw the sting of learning, and to drown in a soft purée the germs of self-awareness and social criticism. Knowledge, made abstract and deprived of the detonator of activity or experience, has lost some of its explosive potential. There are risks in organising schools so that learning opens questions, challenges beliefs and demands action, but it is surely desirable and possible to use power to promote the spirit of enquiry, even into authority itself? There is something almost flippant about those who refuse to tackle these issues, claiming that children work best with the least direction or that curiosity is an inevitable attribute of youth.

Managing diversity

Before comprehensive reorganisation there was little need to analyse or even describe education in managerial terms. Grammar, secondary modern and elementary schools were relatively small, simple and predictable. Two or three forms in each age group followed a lesson pattern that varied little from year to year. Apart from the Head, who appointed teachers and caned pupils, no one managed or supervised anyone else.

Administration and organisation grow more complex by an apparently geometric progression according to the numbers involved. Comprehensives can have up to fifteen forms of entry and well over a hundred teachers; twenty or more subjects at three or four levels of examination may be offered; the diversity of equipment, facilities and people can be almost unlimited. Teachers have had, therefore, to improvise more or less new solutions to problems related to size and diversity, rather than any particular educational strategy. The early comprehensives saw themselves as coming to terms with a plural community, not with discovering a common thread of pedagogic policy.

Comprehensive schools have tended to develop managerial structures to control a self-generated complexity and in general have failed to recognise their own peculiar organisational needs. Heads and staff have been prone to devise elaborate administrative procedures without reference to educational means or ends. For example, elegant timetables, consuming many hours of managerial effort, have been constructed to provide each pupil with a curriculum differentiated according to presumed needs. The principle of individuals and differences dictating a pattern of education is pre-comprehensive; the administrative skills are the only novel contribution and these have been directed towards preserving an archaic curriculum and method. Similarly, pastoral care arrangements have served to promote the smooth running of schools, ensuring that lists are compiled, options selected, careers chosen and registers called. 'Paperwork' began to fill a large proportion of a year tutor's or deputy head's time without necessarily securing any specific comprehensive objective.

Burnham points scores[1] have proved an additional distraction from the questions involved in organising a comprehensive school. Heads have often found themselves engaged in a series of *ad hoc* appointments that have developed an independent logic. As teachers leave the school one by one new staff are engaged. The result can be a collection of individual teachers assigned varying degrees of seniority and a miscellany of tasks to perform, rather than an integrated structure designed to generate opportunities for learning. An organisation based upon an almost accidental pattern of more or less interlocking job descriptions, devised in isolation as vacancies occur, can encourage individuals to work alone on self-contained tasks, needing to be dealt with by reference to routine rather than a shared philosophy or strategy. Schools rarely have the opportunity to plan their structure as a whole, and many still suffer from the effects of decisions forced upon them at the time of reorganisation. This is why new schools can be more experimental and cogent in their comprehensiveness than others.[2]

Diagram 1[3] is an attempt to illustrate some of the difficulties and implications of a number of commonly adopted
management schemes. This 'image of school' suggests the
mental picture shared by many teachers and local authority
officers. A preoccupation with posts of responsibility, the
distribution of status and administrative solutions, strongly
influence how staff visualise their school and its organisation.
Heads sometimes disguise reality, presenting a misleading
picture of how power is distributed or essential issues are
decided in their own establishment. Diagrams in staff handbooks frequently include many overlapping circles, reflecting
a desire for a liberal style and atmosphere. It is as if there were
something impolite about an accurate description of the lines
of authority in action. Schools seem anxious to soften the hard
outlines of hierarchy but find themselves unable to escape
from a management structure similar to that in diagram 1,
shaped like a family tree with the Head as great-grandfather. A
culture of informality is expressed in miscellaneous loops and
arrows while real power flows from above through vertical
lines.

The 'typical' management scheme shown in the diagram
has its origin in the willingness of many Heads to apply their
power and authority to the solution of administrative problems as they arise. Unable to plan a whole structure from a
clear base, Heads impose a coherent arrangement only on
paper, defining in tidy, diagrammatic form a piecemeal allocation of duties.

Diagram 1 reflects a commonplace hierarchical image of
school. Classroom teachers without responsibilities form the
populous base of the pyramid; the Headteacher is at the apex,
unique and without peers. There are perhaps three deputies
(depending on the local authority and the size of the school)
representing 'senior management' and reporting directly to
the Head. 'Middle management' occupies an awkward but
central territory. Many of those who work in a school perceive
its direction in these terms and expect a semi-autocratic exercise of power. At a superficial level the diagram offers a
reasonable portrait of responsibilities, tracing lines of authority and management through the various layers of organisation, indicating who is accountable for what to whom. Areas

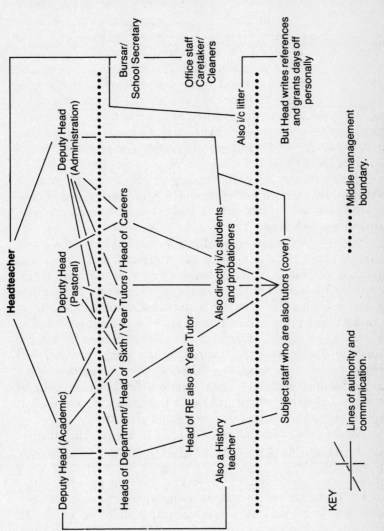

Headteacher

Deputy Head (Administration)

Bursar/
School Secretary

Office staff
Caretaker/
Cleaners

Also i/c litter

But Head writes references
and grants days off
personally

Deputy Head (Pastoral)

Deputy Head (Academic)

Heads of Department/ Head of Sixth / Year Tutors / Head of Careers

Head of RE also a Year Tutor

Also a History teacher

Also directly i/c students
and probationers

Subject staff who are also tutors (cover)

KEY

Lines of authority and
communication.

• • • • • Middle management
boundary.

Diagram 1.   Images of school: a typical management diagram.

of activity (pastoral, academic, administration) are defined and interrelated.

Despite its apparently linear form, the diagram reveals the uncertainties, inconsistencies and ambiguities that bedevil school management. There is a discordance between the linear, pyramidal image shown and the informal, almost casual behaviour noticed by observers and suggested 'between the lines' here. The Head is at the peak of this reporting pyramid, in theory a remote figure dealing only with matters of high policy. Questions should be referred upwards through each 'tier' of management. In practice the lines melt away. The Head teaches Science and reports grades to the head of department, also writing references for every member of staff and bypassing senior and middle managers who are supposed to be responsible for their colleagues. The Head intervenes in day-to-day 'law and order' affairs and assists the caretaker with furniture and litter.

In the model shown, Heads are inclined to behave in a way that diminishes the authority of others and bridges or even short-circuits lines of management. Yet, at the same time, this conduct is a response to a persisting informality of relationships. The Head is caught up in the network of 'ground-floor' connections, protected by few physical or social barriers. The Head can be more powerful than business executives but the form of the pyramid is battered by the social intensity and community consciousness of school life. Conventional images of school, reinforced by a flirtation with line management concepts, repress reality and foster instead an individualised, pluralistic version of responsibility and activity.

Within the boundaries of middle management[4] further confusion distorts the descending line of authority supposedly portrayed. Responsibilities are assigned to individuals as if there were a clear line of communication; in practice duplication of similar tasks and overlapping assignments lead to muddle. The Head of Careers is responsible for a team of teachers; each member of that team also belongs to a subject department and to a parallel set of tutorial staff attached to a year group. Some of the members have separate and independent responsibilities, perhaps for the tuck shop or cycling proficiency. Heads of year are also subject teachers; the Head of RE doubles up as Head of 5th Year. Jobs that are written into individual briefs cannot easily become the subject of teamwork and it is not easy to 'manage' a group of teachers whose loyalties and functions are so frenetically subdivided.

The link between senior staff and heads of year/department is another source of trouble. Middle managers have to report to several members of the senior team while finding juniors in their own departments reporting directly to the deputies. A head of department may provide information about pupils for the Deputy Head (Pastoral) or supply examination details for the Deputy Head (Administration) but there are too many points of cross-reference for efficient line management: a mechanism by which the authority of the deputies is reduced. The coherence of their work is also undermined. The diagram implies a clear job description for each deputy; in practice each is driven to become a progress-chaser, processing information from a wide variety of sources before undertaking an assignment ('the timetable', 'curriculum development') in isolation. There can be no question of leading teams across such ill-defined and complicated boundaries; tasks become a matter of routine and there is no natural structure for change or development. By these means schools solve their day-to-day problems and cope with their hectic diversity; as this analysis suggests, institutional stability is achieved by neglecting or discounting many of the natural impulses of school, which are towards teamwork and informality.

Secondary headship

Many of these difficulties follow from the authoritarian nature of headship. A typical 'articles of government'[5] defines school organisation in relation to the Head whose powers are given a prime ministerial character. The potentially limiting, constraining or inhibiting partners in the service[6] have insufficient strength to oppose successfully a determined Headteacher.

Unless there is some impropriety, Heads hold office for life and can persist with chronically unsatisfactory management methods. Schools are not designed to allow for an alternative source of energy. Parents, staff and pupils can protest and complain but cannot force a change of direction. Governors possess considerable power in theory but in practice use it only in a grave crisis. They lack a method by which the school can be influenced without professional cooperation. If governors overrule a decision[7] it is not easy to implement another policy. Lay people lack time, expertise, information or even the independent advice necessary to form an alternative judgement or opinion.

There are quiet pressures towards conformity and caution but schools still depend upon the Head's initiatives or the lack of them. Final decisions about structure and participation (or, indeed, about anything) are taken by a single individual. This has the advantage of concentrating effective power so that schools can achieve a great deal without outside help or authority, but it also has the disadvantage of converting responsibility into a gift, conferred from above, perhaps on a whim that may not last. Each new Head has to reinvent a structure of delegation (perhaps like that in diagram 1) to avoid the danger of improvising both tactical and strategic decisions with scant reference to colleagues. However it is designed, the structure remains personal and grows from the nature of the institution only during the period of office of a discerning Headteacher.

The deployment of staff and the designation of posts shows the extent of a Head's power. The governors and local education authority have considerable notional responsibility but in shire counties Heads can effectively control appointments and promotions. Urban authorities allow less freedom but there remains extensive scope for diplomacy and 'behind the scenes' manipulation. No one else can repair the damage if Heads fail to consult with colleagues or to calculate the consequences of various decisions. Senior professionals can offer advice but lack authority; visiting inspectors or governors have insufficient information. Much depends on the individual Head's awareness of the combination of opportunities available. For example, the promotion of the Head of English can influence three or four other posts if skilfully managed. Timing is often essential in securing the maximum advantage from circumstances; schools can miss out because the Head does not calculate enough or is insufficiently aware to make the right decisions.

The Burnham structure of graded posts reinforces authority at every stage. A Head controls the agenda and membership of meetings as well as the circulation of information (from staffing and finance to pupil numbers) and personally directs the work of the office staff. The cumulative effect of so much control is very great. Staffing, promotions, timetable and finance, when taken together, offer potential leverage sufficient for any despot. The ascendancy of the centre is further enhanced by the fragmentation of secondary schools into subject departments and the sometimes contrasting requirements of the pastoral system.

There is an additional underlying psychological effect that powerfully underpins authority. People are subconsciously influenced by the idea of an invisible, all-seeing eye, a recreation at work of the parent–child relationship. Teachers and pupils alike feel observed and sense that they earn praise and blame by different types of conduct. School is a public stage and staff have the sense of acting out a role, their behaviour monitored by an unseen eye. There are totalitarian implications in this idea and a number of Heads seem to have based a cult of personality upon it. As in all systems dependent upon leaders, questions of image and meaning become entangled. The independence of teachers and taught is subtly diminished.

Charismatic figures like Rhodes Boyson (while at Highbury Grove) or Peter Dawson (in his time at Eltham Green) are to be expected from a system that charges single individuals with the task of defining and maintaining a network of relationships. Teachers are relieved of the need to make decisions by the exceptional ability of their leaders. It is assumed that the school's values and frame of reference should flow from above. There is great scope here for arbitrary rule and *ad hoc* decisions; a constant temptation to create exceptions and special cases within the shell of one's own rules.

The stifling effect of wise men is rarely reported in their legends. If a Head commands a school by force of personality, some staff may conclude that many matters are not their concern. Heads of department, persuaded of the mystique of the timetable and perhaps the timetabler, may sense that their own role in the proceedings is to give information and advice, almost as bystanders. One management model, known as a 'cascade', provides a suggestive image of initiatives descending from above and perhaps drowning those below whose opportunities for delegation are more restricted. A Head-teacher's pre-eminence can be set against the very citizenship that schools should foster. Paternalistic images of sheep and shepherds are scarcely compatible with democratic objectives. Some schools have achieved, nevertheless, a remarkable level of teamwork and participation. Their example keeps alive the hope that despite the temptations of overwhelming authority Heads can discover a mode of organisation through which to lead their colleagues towards partnership and self-government.

Management science

Impressed by the muddled state of school organisation, many educationists have turned to management consultants in the hope of discovering a scientific method by which matters may be improved. Regional management centres have encouraged local authorities to regard organisation as a technical business to be approached through case studies and theoretical models. Books on the subject contain many diagrams and checklists, describing in detail ideal procedures for every event from a departmental meeting to a timetable.[8] Education for Industrial Society offers a formula for success found attractive by many in education.[9] As with the work of United States business schools, the evidence of applied success is limited except in areas such as accountancy, where manipulation of tax arrangements can yield valuable dividends. This has not affected the popularity of business science as a discipline.

Models of management based on industrial experience have a hard leading edge, pressing individuals to perform effectively by techniques themselves apparently sensible and realistic. Each member of the workforce is assigned a clear place within a formal structure, making explicit who reports to whom about what. Responsibilities are identified precisely

and each individual is made to feel the maximum account-
ability for defined tasks. There is an implied day of judgement
for each manager, when account shall be rendered for budgets,
products and mistakes. People are expected to achieve set
targets or explain failure. Formal reporting mechanisms and
the identification of duties in precise terms are designed to
concentrate the reluctant mind.

Apparently softer messages, stressing 'consultation' and
'participation', in fact support the same object of enhanced
performance and output. Industrial managers are interested in
more democratic forms of organisation only to reduce costs
and increase production and do not intend to surrender control
over the manufacturing process. People are 'involved' only as
an effective means of reaching goals generated through a line
management structure. Most employees in large-scale enterprises are occupied mainly in carrying out instructions issued
by someone else.

This approach may be appropriate for business but is
inimical to an open, flexible, cooperative education. Teachers
and pupils work best in an atmosphere of freedom and trust;
imagination does not flourish where there is frequent or
intrusive inspection. Schools or local authorities that borrow
from industry, seeking greater clarity about methods and
objectives, could find themselves pursuing artificial, if self-
imposed, targets. 'Management' models suffer from the same
limitations as other hierarchical structures. The application of
management science to a clumsy pyramid, like that shown in
diagram 1, might exacerbate rather than resolve organisational
difficulties. Authoritarian systems are designed to provide a
sequence of orders, incentives and supervision on the assumption that workers lack the understanding and commitment to
function without them. Management approaches that stress a
descending line of authority are likely to inhibit the vital
contributions upon which worthwhile learning depends.

Schools resemble industry in bringing together and organising large numbers of people; but learning is an extraordinary activity not easily compared with processes in business or manufacturing. Education has no output or result,
only the possibility of influencing the memory and thoughts of
children. There are no simple relationships between subject,

object and product (as in making something), only continuing conversation, discussion and argument. Senior and junior teachers are engaged in a similar discourse. For example, Heads discuss activities and seek to improve the quality of lessons but teaching is itself a discussion. A school has meetings and systems of communication but these take the form of talk about potential dialogue. Learning is an intangible, complex web of exchanges, not a task performed or a productive act completed. School objectives can be stated in general terms but children retain messages and recollections far from those intended and relationships within a group transform what is learned. The curriculum is the beginning of an experience, not its specification or blueprint. Schools are concerned, therefore, with interrelationships, talk and activity for their own sake. In education, management should be understood as a means of contributing a fresh dimension to a conversation, not as a mechanism for prescribing, defining and arranging tasks.

Rather than imitate industrial practice, Heads and teachers need to devise a management method that enhances the confidence, participation and contribution of every member of the learning community. In the common school, authority should be applied to stimulate questions, prompt discussion and foster partnership, not to secure obedience or to discourage criticism. This is incompatible with a strategy that seeks to describe tasks and objectives in order to check that everyone is following instructions with due urgency. Management in school should instead encourage teachers and children to take responsibility for their activities, to ensure that authority and power are distributed evenly throughout the system. Groups of children cannot be expected to organise themselves and their activities if the structure of the school is designed to ensure that individuals complete specified operations.

Heads are not helped towards such an understanding of school organisation by present arrangements, with their stress upon authority. The prospects for reform are bleak. The example of the Taylor Report[10] on school governors shows how difficult it is to change constitutional arrangements in local authorities. After long research and debate, legislation has taken a different course and years have passed without obvious consequences. Current pressures seem likely to lead to more rather than less authoritarian schemes of management.

Even if there were broader support for new initiatives there is the risk that a fully developed system of democratic control might politicise rather than improve schools, creating the atmosphere of C. P. Snow's Cambridge, with competing interest groups canvassing for particular preoccupations or appointments. The necessarily unequal standing of parents and pupils in the enterprise could compromise the hoped-for partnership. Parents are ill-placed to take an objective view of professional questions in which they are not expert. They have expectations conditioned by their own schooldays, perhaps an inappropriate base from which to judge issues. Parents and pupils should not decide promotions; devising a scheme weighted to give parents a voice without undermining the teacher contribution would not be easy. Cabals of teachers controlling various committees could be equally unwelcome. Schools could be divided, muddled or otherwise disrupted as one group or another established control. Local party caucuses might dictate events despite the intention of reformers to make the community responsible for its own educational facilities. Political wheeling and dealing could displace professional expertise without much deepening the roots of decisions or involvement.

Teachers are as doubtful as parents and a wider public about schools in which pupils decide everything for themselves. The trend is, rather, towards a reduction in the degree of local freedom and autonomy. A more prescriptive curriculum and restricted finance will limit rather than extend the scope for self-determination. Schools are small enough to need something like the potential authority of Headteachers; the destruction of a school's effectiveness is too high a price to pay for what might become a parody of local government.

Yet the potential for reform lies embedded in aspects of contemporary school experience. Provided power is not concentrated at the apex of the pyramid there is continued scope for local leadership and control. While sufficient authority remains within the school there is the possibility of sharing and partnership. Teachers are already anxious to be involved in policy decisions; few education professionals commend an autocratic style or expect it to lead to good results. Heads themselves are used to an informal culture in which agreement is sought. In many schools Heads have demonstrated how much can be achieved within present constitutional arrangements, recognising that the principal leadership task is to foster the self-development of others. Continued progress depends, however, on schools recognising that teamwork and delegation are principles of organisation that need to be systematically applied, not cheerful aspirations to be written in the open spaces of diagram 1.

Alternative networks

An alternative organisational network is suggested in diagram 2. This scheme aims to develop and draw together in a coherent whole the largest possible number of team and group activities, extending responsibility and participation so that decisions can be taken close to the classroom by the teachers involved. The tasks listed in the diagram (column 1) are those upon which school structure is normally based. Each is subdivided for allocation to individuals. The attempt to distribute assignments through a hierarchy after this fashion (cf. diagram 1) is an ineffectual form of delegation, unlikely to lead to the creation of teams or to involve a significant number of colleagues. For example, a deputy head to whom 'discipline' is entrusted may interpret this to mean dealing with cases referred upwards by year tutors, rather than leading and coordinating pastoral activity. Another, responsible for maintenance, may become a repair man, occasionally telephoning contractors but rarely working with and through section heads.

To achieve an efficient pattern of delegation, senior management should create teams to deal with related subjects rather than subdivide tasks into individual assignments. A deputy and two senior teachers[11] might, for example, be responsible for appointments, promotions and in-service training. Heads of department will be seconded to the team from time to time according to the vacancy or subject under consideration. A deputy responsible for collating budget

1. TASKS	2. TEAMS	3. COMMUNICATIONS	4. GROUPS (Members selected from)	5. ACTIVITIES (examples only)
Staffing; promotions, appointments, development and training	▶	Briefing; information and opinion presented to whole staff by Head or deputies	▶ whole staff	Teaching and learning; preparing lessons
Timetable; curriculum development, resources and special needs	▶	Management team; planning, initiating, coordinating activities following from tasks as they arise	▶ senior staff	Counselling and guiding; interviews, writing reports, assemblies
Finance and budget; maintenance, fittings, cleaning, caretaking	▶ The Head, Deputy Heads and senior teachers will form teams of two or three for each task, ensuring activity develops. Other staff may be coopted as required	Heads of Subject/Year; general discussion meeting with Head and/or other members of management team	▶ heads of section and assistants	Curriculum review and evaluation; planning new courses, writing new syllabuses
Assessment and evaluation; tests, quality control	▶	Open meeting; agenda for staff ideas, complaints and suggestions	▶ whole staff	Directing school play or concert; certificate evening or art exhibition
Pastoral care; coordination, duties, discipline, liaison with external agencies	▶	Working parties; ad hoc meetings to develop change – interested teachers or representatives of areas affected	▶ open membership	Parent Staff Association events
Community; adult programme, youth, primary links and liaison, careers, local industry	▶	Meetings with parents, primary heads, officers governors (and sub-committees) as required	▶ school staff and 'outsiders'	Setting up 16+ consortium with other schools

Diagram 2. School network.

estimates prepared by departments may 'double' as a member of the timetable team, considering the wide resource implications of a proposal for curriculum development. He or she could also be a member of the group deciding priorities for ordering new furniture and equipment. Two senior teachers might jointly coordinate the tutorial teams but share too in timetabling or assessment.

A number of senior staff will be responsible for monitoring and initiating action in relation to each group of tasks in column 1. The interlocking activities of senior management replace an elaborate structure of individual jobs as the means by which teachers are involved in policy and decisions.

These 'leader' teams (column 2), comprising senior staff, will set up groups (column 4) to carry out activities (column 5). Some of these will be continuous and require a permanent establishment (e.g. subject departments to organise teaching); others will have a short lifespan (e.g. drafting a new report form or designing an assembly format). In each case the management team as a whole will decide in discussion how each function is perceived and which colleagues should contribute. Small groups form a 'task force' for each activity. Section heads should not be left to deal with responsibilities in isolation, partly because small groups work more efficiently and partly because the nature of the activity is changed by teamwork. The curriculum ceases to present itself as distinct from pastoral care when year tutors are present to point out that behavioural problems often arise from inappropriate or unstimulating teaching. New courses should not be planned without due consideration by those responsible for finance and timetabling.

The intention is to involve teachers in the school's developing policy, raising everyone's performance by emphasising teams and interacting groups working on common projects. A network of connections is set up through which ideas and information may be shared and used. Each group needs the freedom and opportunity for the widest possible discussion. When plans and reports are complete they should, so far as possible, be supported and carried into effect. The original brief or terms of reference for working parties should be precise and specific.

All groups not in permanent commission should be led by a member of the management team so that work can be more easily monitored and related to the whole. Where a keenly interested individual outside the management team is responsible for a group, care must be taken to ensure that progress is integrated with other relevant activities. The Head of 3rd Year might, for example, lead a working party to review the option system or the guidance offered pupils before choices are made. At each stage senior staff coordinating pastoral care and timetabling need to be aware of the discussion and its likely implications. It is inevitable, however, that scaled posts of responsibility outside the management team should be allocated to teachers leading permanent groups. Each head of subject/area/year is the natural leader of three or four teachers, planning and organising their work together.

Communications

The complex activities of so many related groups need to be planned, integrated and controlled through a sophisticated communication system (column 3). When small project teams replace a sequence of individualised assignments a school's meetings become an essential clearing house through which disparate tasks and events are set in motion, scheduled and related.

Each of the six main types of meeting shown in column 3 serves a separate but related function. There is, for example, a substantial difference between a briefing at which explanation and information are disseminated and a small working party concerned to review a particular development. If members do not properly appreciate a meeting's purpose, considerable frustration can be caused. The variety of forms of information drawn together in the context of a meeting increase the possibility of misunderstanding. Written notes, letters, discussion papers, reports, proposals, memoranda, bulletins and even conversation pose their distinctive difficulties. The following principal media for communication are distinguished in diagram 2.

Briefing

The Head or deputies provide information and explanation of day-to-day events for the staff as a whole. The aim is to avoid confusion, uncertainty and false report as well as to foster corporate feeling. Dates for the completion of various operations will be announced and progress on routine matters will be 'chased'.

Management team

Aims and objectives need to be set and reviewed regularly so that progress can be assessed and the place of individual projects monitored and determined. The Head has a particular responsibility to ensure that senior staff collaborate so that sufficient authority, time, space, resources and personnel are available to the individual or team asked to perform specified tasks. Management will seek the smooth integration of activities and impose deadlines where appropriate.

Heads of subject/year

Heads of section are concerned with originating and carrying into effect a wide range of regular or routine tasks; frequent meetings are necessary to schedule and coordinate work that might otherwise become fragmented. Pastoral and subject leaders should be brought together for regular discussion of common problems. The aim is to publicise, discuss, confirm or amend proposals or ideas originating in smaller meetings, and to provide a forum at which a decision may be finally agreed and ratified. Faculties or departments should not become the school's structure by default. Groups functioning in isolation swiftly lose momentum and direction.

Open meeting

Staff attend on a voluntary basis and can offer agenda items. Complaints, suggestions and controversies are aired so that conflicting feelings and reactions may be talked through. The meeting is intended to cultivate a shared purpose and to ensure that the system is responsive to the ebb and flow of opinion.

Working parties

Working parties provide the consultative mechanism through

which the teams (column 2) and groups (column 4) can discuss and disseminate preliminary proposals for change or seek opinions about existing practice before developing new ideas. Membership should combine a representative element with the participation of those most interested and willing to contribute.

Meeting with outsiders

Senior staff are likely to coordinate the contributions of parent and governor subcommittees, and to conduct discussions with relevant external agencies. Results should be reported in an open forum (e.g. briefing, heads of section).

This pattern of communication, designed to support group activity at every level, can degenerate into aimless talk unless a single, named person accepts designation as an executive, responsible for achieving each objective and ensuring that work is completed according to a schedule decided in advance by the management team. When there is a considerable degree of delegation it is necessary to locate responsibility with high precision if groups are to perform effectively. This is quite unlike the pressure applied to individuals, against their will, in a line management setting.

These proposals suggest a strategy through which Heads can work to promote self-confidence, increased responsibility and more broadly based decision-making within existing schools. Skilful leadership can be the starting point for change, rather than an inhibiting focus of authority. Schools organised in this way will foster relationships quite different from those of the lecture room. People will be drawn into the activities of the place and will have scope to explore and experiment on their own initiative. A framework will be established within which the learning experience can be profoundly altered.

Teachers who are nurtured, stimulated and perhaps stretched by working in a lively team will approach their pupils with changed expectations. Staff whose commitment and enthusiasm are assiduously cultivated may be prepared to undertake an open and adventurous journey. Few of us improve when corrected, rebuked or punished. It is in our power to create a new climate for democratic education.

CHAPTER 4

The sceptred curriculum

At first glance, curriculum planning seems an infinitely open-ended activity, with so many choices to be made between beguiling possibilities. In reality existing staffing, tradition and resources constrain the least adventurous school. A curriculum is sometimes little more than the sediment left from appointments made over a period of twenty years or more, reflecting the successive exigencies of emergency training, mature entrants, subject shortages, the 'all-graduate profession' and, recently, redundancy. Teachers have matured in their posts and entertain fixed expectations, whether or not the Department of Education and Science (DES) or Her Majesty's Inspectors (HMI) publish proposals or recommendations. A plan for the curriculum maze must take account of this reality if ordinary children are to be 'trained differently' and given the 'souls of kings and queens'.

What do children need to know before they can 'wield the royal sceptre' and exercise the critical independence of self-governing citizens? How should the curriculum be arranged to develop 'arrogance' as well as understanding? A fundamental shift is required, from a curriculum varied to meet the different needs of individuals, towards common, shared activities. What children experience together is the foundation for their future citizenship.

Relevance and vocation

First-generation comprehensives offered a plural curriculum to meet the supposed needs of diverse groups of pupils. The new schools adopted a dualist model in which 'academic' pupils studied languages and sciences while 'practical' pupils followed extended courses in woodwork and painting. Curriculum content was varied from band to band to allow for varying degrees of academicism or practicality, determined by reference to eleven-plus scores disproportionately influenced by intelligence tests. 'Flying' sets were entered a year early for GCE while the small grouping of 'less able' pupils supposedly aided those with learning difficulties. Children's future employment in clerical or manual occupations overshadowed their lessons while their shared community identity and responsibilities were discounted.

Schools have become increasingly uneasy about general categories and labels, however. Many are now reluctant to draw sharp lines between subjects or pupils. Major publications[1] have supported progress towards a common curriculum. Other central government manoeuvres, like the legislation on special education following the Warnock Report,[2] or projects sponsored by the Manpower Services Commission (MSC), have generated a contrary pressure to respond to 'special needs' and occupational imperatives, particularly in technology. A curriculum adjusted to individual needs and differences should, nevertheless, be resisted on practical and philosophical grounds. Additional teaching or expensive equipment has to be funded by worsening conditions elsewhere. Small, specialised groups or individual tutorials designed to assist minorities cause a corresponding deterioration in the experience offered everyone else.

The cost of variations in class size can be illustrated by comparing the 96 teachers required to teach 800 pupils in groups of 10 for a week with the 38.4 staff needed for the same students organised in groups of 25. To accommodate remedial lessons the numbers in Art or Science lessons may have to be increased to the point where worthwhile practical activity may be seriously impaired. The resulting stress for pupils and teachers may stimulate further demand for special treatment. The benefits for those whose special needs are provided for have to be weighed against the hidden loss of quality in other classrooms. A majority of pupils, not qualifying for help, may find their elementary need for reasonable working space in laboratories and workshops denied.

Remedial departments, or special schemes like the Technical and Vocational Education Initiative, are open to the same criticism as Educational Priority Areas (EPAs). There are as many, or perhaps more, disadvantaged students widely scattered in neighbouring districts as there are living within a designated EPA. Indiscriminate aid is given to everyone within priority areas, whether or not it is needed, while nothing is offered elsewhere. Similarly, remedial teachers can give personal attention in small groups, while in every class two or three students, indistinguishable from those receiving special care, are neglected. A further problem is establishing the criteria by which pupils are selected. Measures of ability and aptitude are insufficiently reliable to decide which children would most benefit from individual help. Sometimes disruptive behaviour earns attention while serious learning difficulties are overlooked.

However pupils are selected, as many in need can be excluded as receive assistance. If the gifted, the less able, the disruptive, slow learners and ethnic minorities all received additional support, the momentum of the main curriculum would be dissipated amongst many diversions, leaving little energy for the main task. A properly designed, well-taught curriculum for all may be a more effective remedy than a constant effort to devise adequate 'elastoplast' for a multitude of deficiencies. Conversely, if the whole school curriculum is appropriate for a minority, it is likely to be satisfactory for everyone. Schools are not designed to deal with problems individually and the most carefully planned setting or banding can leave groups where many children need help. Sometimes small groups are essential and well justified, but it is impractical to adopt the meeting of individual needs as a curriculum principle. Teachers should ensure, rather, that the initial design is sufficiently comprehensive, so that the opportunities for pursuing particular interests do not undermine a general diversity and richness. Should a small, expensive photography group, for example, be funded at the expense of line or clay work for everyone?

The principal objection to a plural curriculum relevant to future employment is not, however, practical. In a democratic society comprehensive schools have an obligation to offer access to a wide range of experiences and an enlarged understanding. As many people as possible should be enabled to choose, or at least contribute towards the taking of decisions and the framing of goals. There is an almost awesome presumption about those who seek to prescribe in advance the purposes and future of groups and individuals, channelling young lives towards specific, seemingly relevant skills and techniques. Citizenship depends upon general understanding, not specialised training based on premature assumptions about pupils' potential. Whatever sources of knowledge and insight are available should be open to all. The curriculum should comprise a structure of experiences designed to establish as many reference points as possible for encounters with ideas, people and events after school years. Training operatives and technicians is another business entirely.

The example of micro-technology is instructive. In a fit of economic panic governments have subsidised a massive investment in a very narrow sector of the high-tech equipment market; it would be as reasonable to supply every child with a musical instrument, in the hope of displacing the United States from its dominance of western light entertainment or enhancing the competitiveness of the London Philharmonic. The economic consequences of such an investment are incalculable but the prospects of success are dim. Are there sufficient teachers (of the violin? of programming? of the oboe? of semi-conductor technology?) to make effective use of the equipment? Is the structure of the British economy such that it could usefully deploy huge numbers of programmers or musicians?

If the future lies in computing, firms will train their employees accordingly, but the image of millions of workers programming computers for purposes as yet undefined is an unconvincing one. The attempts to make education self-consciously useful are likely to prove a failure; needs-related training is plainly distinct from education, which must always be open-ended and broadly based. As manufacturing declines and youth unemployment reaches 50 per cent there is even less justification than before for an instrumental view of schooling. Furthermore, perhaps ironically, the well-planned general education necessary for citizenship may also prove, in the slightly longer run, the best form of vocational preparation. Flexibility and open-mindedness have become invaluable virtues.

Relevance and practical applications should not, however, be discounted in the context of curriculum planning. Linkages with employment and the community represented by work experience, social service, industrial visits, business simulations and other schemes should be a natural extension of the concept of a general education. Vocational experiences should function as a reality principle, bringing youngsters into contact with the life and work of their neighbourhood. Twenty years ago, and in some schools still, typical thirteen-year-olds would have had more idea of the economic life of Nigeria than of their own city.

The community can be the starting point of school, where an understanding of economic and social processes can be grounded in local events and culture. Working in a factory can be as educational as a theoretical study of nineteenth-century factory legislation. The educational purpose of such studies is an understanding of work and society, not the job-specific or even generic 'training' criticised earlier. Liberal education is not in itself relevant or irrelevant; the point is, rather, that education needs to develop through practical application if it is to be an effective medium for coming to terms with the world. Lessons should be related to everyday things and pupils need to be introduced to concepts through applications that are part of local experience and culture.

A vocational or pre-vocational approach can be rejected only if a sense of purpose and reality is a characteristic feature of school study. In Mathematics, for example, ideas should be applied so that pupils can see how concepts and activities relate to one another. Teaching the proofs of Euclidian geometry without reference to their use is as unsatisfactory as an attempt to prime school leavers with basic arithmetic as specified by engineering employers. Meaning, not usefulness, is the essential criterion for measuring relevance.

Specialisation

A common curriculum does not, however, resolve the problems caused by a relentless, progressive specialisation *within* subjects of study offered to all pupils. Specialisation fosters diversity, encourages differences and devalues ordinary experience. There are many casualties as the years pass; children lose their curiosity because learning has moved to a plane of specialised abstraction beyond the scope of common sense. A successful few, selecting individual paths through Ordinary and Advanced level GCE, themselves become experts, managers of modern society set apart from their community and fellows. Accountants, computer programmers, lawyers, civil servants, mathematicians and physicists fall from the colander, final products to justify a system of learning.

The pressure of the universities, examination syllabuses, the 'qualification spiral' and teachers' own experience of higher education gradually squeezes out real life. An increasingly special and specific knowledge is introduced, unrelated to phenomena or events within range of a child's senses. Subjects are based on a remote world with its own structure and logic, a vast corpus of specialised material that it is felt young scientists or historians 'should' know. Children's own knowledge and language are progressively eliminated as suitable subjects for study and discussion. Text-books adopt a bland, neutral, descriptive formula, encouraging students to depend on authority and memory rather than on mental or physical activity. Controversy and dialogue are bleached out like stains from pure linen. Secondary schools with their 'facilities' and departments are temples built for experts who zealously guard the secrets of specialism. Schools that experiment with integrated schemes, seeking to create interdisciplinary teams sharing 'skills', swim against the tide of teacher education and professional development. Few are prepared to hazard their public esteem by a radical departure from single-subject examinations at CSE or GCE level so that movements towards integration have constantly to struggle with the inherent logic of the education system.

Children of all abilities are often (if not generally) taught topics at a level beyond the scope of non-specialist teachers. How many staff could, for example, achieve a satisfactory grade on the School Mathematics Project (SMP) paper? What results would teachers themselves record on CSE papers outside their own area? Subjects apparently less abstract in form and method are examined as if the aim were to discourage further study. Only specialists have sufficient confidence or 'expertise' to deal with elaborate secret codes, minute detail and an obsession with technique. Teachers of long standing feel threatened by new turns of the screw in their specialism, (for example, the 'New' Geography) which seem to transform familiar symbols into a foreign language. Few staff are now willing or able to perform as general subjects teachers and their reluctance indicates the extraordinary, fragmented, highly specialised menu offered from an early point in secondary schools. Children are asked to count metaphorical angels on the head of a pin, but the fish and dogs that they like pass unobserved.

In Science, for example, syllabuses were increasingly overloaded and over-specialised as knowledge grew in Physics, Chemistry and Biology. The Nuffield Foundation funded a major curriculum development designed to reduce the emphasis on content by focusing upon the essential concepts and processes underlying scientific understanding. Children were encouraged to experiment and investigate for themselves. While Nuffield succeeded in establishing new, practically based methods of Science teaching, the undergraduate student of Physics or Chemistry has remained the fixed reference point for Science syllabuses and examinations. Nuffield did not redefine the appropriate content of the curriculum, in some ways increasing the burden on students and teachers by demanding understanding as well as facts. The result is that teachers still despair of 'covering' the syllabus and worry that a combined Nuffield approach in the junior years may leave too much to do in years four, five and six. Lessons have to accelerate onwards before essential ideas have been absorbed, hastening from the concrete and particular towards the abstract and general, every pupil receiving a training necessary only for those planning a career in Science. This pace, and the emphasis on breadth of coverage rather than on an understanding of general principles, is crippling for many students who are bemused by the number and variety of concepts thrust before them. There is no time for speculation, discovery or experimentation; learning becomes an obstacle course, a roundabout rotating ever more quickly. Discussion, group work, and time-consuming points arising spontaneously from investigations are progressively excluded as the secondary years pass.

The worst effects of detailed, specialist study are exacerbated by a number of prejudices derived from the days when certain subjects and activities achieved high status through their association with the grammar school. Writing and criticising are valued highly; talking and doing are discouraged. The critical, scholarly apparatus and the standard, authoritative commentators and texts are slavishly admired and copied. Status as well as utilitarianism explains why Mathematics traditionally occupies five times as much timetable space as Art. The balance of the familiar curriculum or even that recommended in such publications as *A Framework for the School Curriculum*[3] makes no allowance for children or teaching, only for the alleged requirements of putative employers. The preference for technique and detail is carried to such lengths that real life almost disappears beneath a patina of fine critical points. The moral or human questions in literature are sometimes omitted in favour of memorising the plot or mastering a linguistic subtlety. Feelings are almost taboo; major issues of politics, religion or sex are considered unsuitable or unsafe.

The problem lies less in the subjects themselves than in the choice of a microscope to aid the selection of topics. Once beneath the lens, an immense variety of detail is revealed upon specimens and is added to the syllabus. Lessons cover ground rapidly and ability comes to be defined in terms of speed in processing quantities of information. Education has moved a long way from the 'natural' learning of Rousseau and even further from children's experiences. Some specialisation is inevitable and advances knowledge: particularly in Science and Mathematics expert teaching is often necessary and contributes to the strength of secondary education; pottery, cookery, silkscreen printing or French conversation are further examples of beneficial specialisation.

Subjects are, in practice, what teachers collectively decide to make them. They are taught, on the whole, as current theories and resources permit. Geography, for example, is a remarkable interdisciplinary discipline, bringing together the insights of the natural and human sciences. Its effective curriculum contribution will be more or less specialised according to the topics selected and the way they are taught. Merging Geography in a Humanities scheme may or may not be desirable but will not necessarily ensure that items are selected so that children can relate to them more easily. A teacher compelled to consider a panoramic view of human knowledge and to exercise a cross-curricular responsibility for communication skills or mathematical development is no more likely to prepare an accessible or less specialised lesson. What are commonly described as 'academic subjects' can be studied in an intensely practical, thought-provoking manner and can be closely connected to the life and experiences of children without their seriousness, purpose or place in the curriculum being in any sense compromised.

Subjects or skills?

Inspectors, civil servants, ministers and curriculum innovators have been united in criticising a single-subject approach. They have deeply regretted schools' preoccupation with content for its own sake, premature specialisation, artificial choices for pupils and the thoughtless accumulation of facts. The attempt to construct a curriculum according to wider principles or criteria other than those associated with traditional subjects is, however, fraught with rarely acknowledged difficulty. The Assessment of Performance Unit (APU) has helped popularise the idea of 'areas of experience' and 'lines of development',[4] while successive DES publications have encouraged teachers to talk in terms of skills, attitudes, personal qualities and learning behaviours. A 'skills' curriculum seems within the reach of those brave enough to abandon the 'compartments' of single subjects. The aim is to escape some of the consequences of specialisation and to recover elements of understanding and activity from the mindless rote learning so often observed in schools.

Unfortunately, as suggested above,[5] there are philosophical and practical problems in defining the thought processes involved in learning and deducing a curriculum map from them. The enumeration of skills can lead to an unsatisfactory catalogue of definitions overlapping with one another and open to a variety of subjective interpretations. The Oxford English Dictionary, for example, describes 'imagination' as the 'Action of imagining, or forming a mental concept of what is not actually present to the senses' or 'the creative faculty' or 'thought, opinion'. 'Creativity' is, however, 'the action of making, forming, producing or bringing into existence'. 'Design' is the 'adaption of means to ends' or 'A plan or scheme conceived in the mind of something to be done'. 'Analysis' leads towards another form of confusion, denoting 'the resolution of a chemical compound into its proximate or ultimate elements' as well as 'Literature. The critical examination of any production, so as to exhibit its elements in simple form'. These notions do not greatly aid the selection of teaching topics or help the teacher decide upon an appropriate emphasis in looking at the carbon cycle or Homer's *Iliad*.

Coltham and Fines's attempt to devise objectives for History[6] is an example of the dangers of this approach. Gard and Lee's critique[7] concludes that: 'precise objectives of the kind required by Coltham and Fines are (at least) extremely difficult to formulate in history, and indeed their value and attainability is a matter for doubt in a wide range of disciplines'.[8] Gard and Lee are particularly severe because Coltham and Fines see 'imagination in emotional terms as an intuitive "power", or faculty' and are therefore unable 'consistently to distinguish between "empathy", "sympathy", "involvement" and "identification"'.[9]

Gard and Lee are right to suspect that 'objectives' are more useful for assessment than curriculum planning. The APU has been anxious to emphasise processes and understanding rather than prescribe content that teachers might interpret as an embryo DES syllabus. In Science, for example, monitoring teams are investigating six 'Categories of Science Performance', including children's ability to conduct experiments, form hypotheses or observe. Broadly 'political' considerations,[10] together with a Nuffield-like interest in activity and method, have led the APU to define Science as a sequence of 'process propositions'. HMI seem to believe that a generalised version of these might constitute a 'line' of scientific development crossing a range of subjects from History to Home Economics and represent an alternative principle for drafting a curriculum.

The old idea that children's learning depends upon intrinsic intellectual qualities[11] that can be measured without reference to experience or content reinforces this renewed interest in 'thinking skills'. Content is considered a separate, almost subsidiary issue. Processes and skills, however, soon lose their meaning when detached from appropriate content. Empathy has no significance unless applied to a child's experience of Charles I; when the content is *King Lear* something else may happen, but it all rather depends on the student, the teacher and the context. Similarly, 'analysis' may describe the precise examination of Hitler's moves in 1939 or the application of food tests; the philosophical discussion of the student's state of mind is most unlikely to clarify what is experienced. The logical development of the curriculum cannot be sustained on such a vague and ambiguous basis.

Process propositions, however carefully drafted to 'cover' the activities it is desired to promote, seem inadequate as a substitute for an established curriculum. Suppose, for example, a cookery lesson could be adapted to give extended practice in scientific skills such as observation and investigation, would it then be acceptable to drop Chemistry and Biology from the timetable? A 'taxonomy' of educational objectives does not, itself, suggest an appropriate content, and leaves the question 'What should we teach?' unanswered. In practice the 'skills' perspective substitutes a philosophical debate over the definition of useful objectives for the value judgements necessary before any scheme of work can be compiled. Teachers cannot easily escape the task of selection by defining objectives independently of the knowledge through which they may be realised. There is an Alice-in-Wonderland flavour to the idea that the reign of Elizabeth I is an obstacle to the development of empathy, or that flora and fauna are a nuisance in a field otherwise reserved for interesting speculation.

The present fashion for over-emphasising skills and thinking may in its turn prove as unhelpful as the unreflecting pursuit of specialised content. It would be ironic if the desire to encourage thoughtful and skilful activity succeeded only in recreating in a new form the division between theory and practice that has contributed in large measure to present difficulties.

Theory and practice

A divided curriculum emerged from the inter-war years and has persisted despite the comprehensive experience. To some extent the diversity of reorganised schools provided a continuing justification for a differentiated curriculum. IQ tests and grammar, elementary and modern schools between them unconsciously moulded a bilateral curriculum, the constituent elements of which have yet to be fully reconciled. Certain subjects developed theoretically; others came to be regarded as practical, concerned with the development of useful physical skills. The division between theory and practice, although modified by the movement towards a common pattern of study in recent years and the development of new teaching methods, remains influential. Parental and pupil attitudes towards Art and Craft in particular are often still shaped by a peculiarly English disdain for doing and making.

There is more at stake, however, than preferences between subjects and their relative status. Traditions of teaching have evolved, leading to an abstract, bookish, verbal mode of instruction in the liberal humanities (e.g. Languages, History, Geography) and an emphasis on practical skills in Metalwork, Woodwork, Cookery, Art and Needlework. The conception that some activities are theoretical and others manual has diminished the scope, meaning and teaching possibilities of

most subjects. The development of Craft, Design and Technology was long delayed by a gloomy, workshop image and
by the belief that it is an area where less able students can learn
how to use tools and make simple objects. Only in the last few
years has an integrated, coherent discipline emerged to show
that sustained thought and planning of a distinctive kind are an
inseparable part of practical activity. Similarly, classroom
subjects have been approached as though facts were their only
connection with experience and activity. Pupils take notes and
learn explanations without any sense that ideas can be tested
against reality or that daily life offers the opportunity for
experiment and investigation.

   Science, a relative latecomer to the school scene, bridged
the divide but suffered from teachers who taught facts and
concepts without conducting experiments or showing the
empirical foundation of their statements. H. G. Wells's father
was an early exponent of 'theoretical' Science:

> And I can quite understand, too, my father's preference for
> what he called an illustrative experiment, which was simply an
> arrangement of the apparatus in front of the class with nothing
> whatever by way of material, and the Bunsen burner clean and
> cool, and then a slow luminous description of just what you did
> put in it when you were so ill-advised as to carry the affair
> beyond illustration, and just exactly what ought anyhow to
> happen when you did. He had considerable powers of vivid
> description, so that in this way he could make us see all he
> described. The class, freed from any unpleasant nervous ten-
> sion, could draw this still life without flinching, and if any part
> was too difficult to draw, then my father would produce a
> simplified version on the blackboard to be copied instead. And
> he would also write on the blackboard any exceptionally
> difficult but grant-earning words, such as 'empyreumatic' or
> 'botryoidal'.[12]

In fairness, Wells senior was influenced by poverty as well as
theory, and later teachers have been similarly constrained by
syllabuses and resources. Nuffield was, nevertheless, an essential reminder that children should learn about Science through
experiments and practical activity of their own. There was an
imminent danger of teachers converting Science into a chiefly
theoretical subject, serving their pupils with facts and conclu-

sions but omitting enquiry. Nuffield succeeded in establishing the pedagogic point that children learn better by 'performing investigations' for themselves than by observing a demonstration, however graphic. Teachers in other subjects have not faced so drastic a challenge and their characteristic teaching style is marked still by a willingness to think of their work as theoretical or practical. This perception is unlikely to be much altered by a rearrangement of subjects within the curriculum.

Teaching method – that is, the activity of pupils and teachers in relation to a prescribed subject – needs to be considered as a separate question; thoughtfulness or practical activity, however defined, cannot be produced by prefacing a list of topics with a grid of skills and processes. Each subject has to earn its place on its own merit as an important contribution to general experience. Its teaching should be planned to interweave theory and practice.

Balance and variety

The first stage in deciding upon a school's teaching programme is to identify the knowledge without which a general experience would be defective. Despite a quarter of a century of educational debate, the curriculum at Stanground and in the other Peterborough schools closely resembles what I remember from Eltham Green. Nothing important has been added or taken away, although the balance of time and topics within and between subjects has varied. Eltham offered an option scheme only slightly more restricting than that now typical. There is more combined work in Science and Humanities but the principal concepts are almost unchanged.

Peterborough schools are probably as different from one another as any one of them is from a London comprehensive in the 1950s. Local conditions possibly have greater curriculum influence than either debate or time. Whilst this is perhaps a sobering perspective for those discussing curriculum philosophy and reform, it is also some indication that there is a settled agreement about what should be taught at school. However subjects are chosen they are no more than instruments through which a broad range of experiences can be organised and presented. Individual topics will be selected according to a teacher's judgement of their importance and value, while their significance for the whole curriculum will depend on how they are learned. Even where content provides a constant source of contrast, comparison and counterpoint there is no guarantee that this will be apparent in the classroom or have the desired effect.

Compromises between what is desirable and what is possible, between various judgements as well as between competing demands for time or resources, are inevitable, even in the most carefully planned curriculum. The claim of any subject, group of subjects, topic or sub-topic must, therefore, be measured against criteria or guidelines. These need not be fixed or rigid, but the following questions are intended to test for the comprehensiveness and accessibility of a proposed scheme.

1. *Does each subject represent a distinctive form of knowledge? What would be lost if it were omitted?*

Schools are continually asked to introduce new subjects, often on the grounds that the addition will be relevant to 'the modern, technological world'. Political Studies, Information Skills, Computer Studies, Social Studies and Economics, amongst others, have been added in numerous schools, provoking critics to complain that the 'secret garden' of the curriculum is overgrown with weeds.

Suppose a secondary school wished to introduce 'Information Skills', drawing together a variety of techniques to support independent learning. Is timetable space available? What can be left out? Is learning how to research more relevant or useful than Music? Can a future be anticipated where children do not study their own language or History? Are less 'useful' subjects doomed? In years one to three the only possibility is to reduce the time for some subjects to create another but this has the side-effect of restricting opportunities in the Humanities, for example, for enquiry methods to be applied. It is interesting that curriculum innovation usually entails displacing History and Geography as self-contained subjects in the first two years, an indication of the fixity of other disciplines. Information Skills is not a distinctive form of knowledge and there is a real danger of duplication. Historians teach the use of evidence and documents; Geography concentrates on maps; Mathematics shows how to draw graphs and charts; English deals with books. In each case the subject already on the curriculum has an abundance of established material to develop 'skills'. It is perhaps a mistake to remedy defects in the teaching of History and Geography by introducing an alternative approach to the same process. The same teachers are likely to repeat their mistakes, if mistakes there are, neglecting the index and failing to show children how to find out or manipulate data.

Schools generally evade a decision to substitute new for old or reduce the time allowed for existing subjects. Instead, Economics, Sociology and other contemporary or relevant enthusiasms are introduced through the option mechanism. Pupils are then free to choose and timetablers remove whatever proves least popular. Computer Studies, for example, is a growth area, recruiting keen students from unspecified rivals.

2. *Is the topic an essential experience for all pupils?*

A useful guide as to whether a subject or topic should be included is its suitability for everyone. No future citizen should be deprived of certain experiences of language, Mathematics and Science; items of mainly specialist interest should be included only if they do not reduce the time available for a whole class to learn fully a topic of central importance.

Some subjects have traditionally been omitted in whole or part for pupils described as 'less able'. This practice is incompatible with the principles of common education. As many as 20 per cent of all students (nationally), for example, study no foreign language, and over 60 per cent do not take an examination course in one. This can partly be explained by a shortage of teachers in the past and the omission of Modern or Ancient Languages from the curriculum of a great many secondary modern schools. Language teaching has, therefore, been concentrated on able or amenable pupils.

The prejudice of the divided system persists in the quiet belief that French or German is essential for higher sets and unimportant for the rest. French has become the ultimate academic subject. This is unacceptable. A case for foreign languages as a distinctive contribution to general understanding can hardly be valid for some pupils but not others. It might be reasonable to request extra time for the least successful students but not to suggest less. In English or Mathematics, by contrast, it is expected that everyone will follow a full five-year course and special provision is made for 'slow learners'. If French does indeed offer a unique insight into language and culture as well as an invaluable parallel and contrast with our own, all pupils should enjoy the benefits. The difficulties of teaching, which may be as great in other disciplines, should not be confused with those of curriculum design.

3. How much time does a subject need to be taught effectively? Can such a claim for time be allowed when balanced against other requests?

The allocation of time to subjects is, in general, arbitrary and is related to tradition, resources and internal politics rather than to a plain curriculum rationale. Mathematics, for example, is disproportionately emphasised to the disadvantage of subjects (Art, Craft, Music) potentially as important. An average pupil may experience three hours per week of Mathematics for five years, while in Music talent has to be developed in one hour per week for three years. This disparity cannot be justified on general educational grounds without an objective gauge for measuring and comparing different subjects or areas of knowledge. The utilitarian case for extended practice in basic arithmetic has to be set against the consideration that the average primary school leaver is sufficiently expert with numbers to meet the 'needs of daily life'. Calculation and rhythm are vital ingredients of life, and children need a full experience of both.

German, Spanish or Italian is necessary for only a few children whose future studies or business will be aided by the acquisition of a second tongue. Another language does not, however, enhance experience derived from the first in proportion to the time consumed, and for this reason is not an appropriate addition for most children. This is a case where the specialised needs of the few must be met provided the 'second language' does not disrupt the common curriculum pattern or become a concealed source of grouping by ability. It would not be right to deny even a few children the opportunity to learn a second language until they are adult.

4. *Is the proposed content appropriate for children? Is the material over-specialised or reliant on over-sophisticated initial concepts and means of communication? Can it be related to the neighbourhood, local culture and language of the children? Does it lead to activity?*

Specialisation superimposes the logic and coherence of a body of knowledge upon the learning needs of children. In a university or even the sixth form this may be necessary, even if it limits enjoyment, but for pupils under sixteen it is lunacy, a sad survival of past ambition. Teachers in secondary education should not offer pre-vocational training for academics after the independent school pattern. They should, rather, prepare young people for life in the local community, enabling them to explore and discover the value of a wide range of concepts and activities.

As the discussion of Nuffield Science has already suggested, the coverage of large numbers of topics and the need to learn a great quantity of information may impede worthwhile learning. Sufficient time to plan and conduct an investigation and follow through some of its implications is much more valuable than a passing, unthought-out acquaintanceship with a much larger number of topics. In History, patches or even individual events or incidents provide a far better basis for understanding than the cavalcade of the past. Effective learning is greatly aided when children can recognise and identify with the people and problems to which they are introduced. Understanding will be assisted if topics are related to every day life and are accessible to common sense.

Experiences need to be built outwards from the student's present position, developing an existing language and method. There are many opportunities for using the local environment that are disregarded on grounds of expense or trouble. Teachers in Geography, for example, often adopt the manner of Wells's father, when they might instead organise a survey, field study or practical enquiry. Topics need to be chosen with half an eye upon the activities that may be derived from or based upon them.

Another unfortunate effect of specialisation is that it enhances the authority of the teacher and reduces the confidence of a pupil faced with abstract or unknown territory. Teachers are more likely to rely upon exposition and description when the subject matter is at the limit of pupils' comprehension. Uncertain of themselves, children lack the confidence for disagreement, experiment or the manipulation of ideas. And yet it is when students are uncertain that they need to find their own language for the concepts to which they are being introduced. *Activity* is the thing most likely to stimulate a constructive response.

5. Has the expertise of present staff or likely appointments been taken into account?

Teachers, not timetables, are the heart of the curriculum. It is essential to consider in detail how a change will develop the strength of individuals and foster effective working teams. Plans that disregard the experience, skills and potential of the staff in pursuit of an artificial framework of predetermined educational objectives will not succeed.

Options

Most schools offer a large number of examination courses, which can be selected through a box or column arrangement to provide fourth- and fifth-year students with an almost personal timetable. Despite recent progress towards a common programme during a 'foundation' phase (usually years one and two), pluralism persists at examination level where less than 30 per cent of the week may be spent on 'core' subjects like English and Mathematics, taken by everyone. In perhaps a majority of schools, areas like Science, Modern Languages, Humanities and Craft are optional so that the effects of differentiation are uncharted. There is a tendency for the familiar 'academic'/'practical', 'able'/'less able' stereotypes to influence the guidance offered by careers and form tutors. At thirteen-plus, children choose themselves for a divided curriculum.

The provision of up to six choices can have a disruptive influence on planning. The number of groups for each subject cannot be predicted with any precision, so that late in the year, when pupil preferences are finalised, considerable adjustments have to be made to take account of fluctuations in demand. An extra option group in a subject where resources are restricted means that teacher deployment in the lower school has to be made more economical without regard to the curriculum needs of those pupils. Option columns traditionally consume a disproportionate share of the school's teaching periods. These features are incompatible with a genuinely comprehensive organisation.

Opportunities for pupils to make decisions are scarce, nevertheless, and should not be rejected out of hand. However, although pupils are encouraged to make critical choices *between* subjects, once inside the lesson they discover a mode of teaching more regimented, specialised and rapid than before.[13] Personal files and projects give some scope for self-directed or independent study but the taught syllabus is extensive and demanding, more or less precluding collaborative or investigative learning styles. Should pupils drop Science or train as a typist at age fourteen? Is it right that subjects should give up pupils with the same combination of despair and relief expressed by the youngsters themselves? By what reasoning is English made compulsory while French and History are dropped by half the age group?

An equitable distribution of time between subjects can ease the task of creating a common curriculum in years four and five, although there are grounds for allowing an element of choice. It is not, after all, practical or even desirable to follow examination courses in all the subject areas studied in years one to three. The attempt to cover too many subjects can aggravate an existing tendency to haste. New subjects and an element of vocational study have to be introduced while additional time for a second language and a second Science has to be found. The main principle of a common curriculum should be sustained but some room must be allowed for taste and interest; there is no overriding objection to a measure of selection *within* existing subject areas.

A common language

A common curriculum provides a basis upon which teachers can begin to take account of the holistic, experiential view of learning described above.[14] No school curriculum can, however, ensure that lessons are conducted in concrete, ordinary language or that a collaborative dialogue is set in motion. On the contrary, developments in English teaching point in another direction: a framework of specific skills is being constructed to ensure that pupils come to terms with the minimum requirements of standard English.

In the 1960s a generation of English teachers, influenced by David Holbrook's *English For Maturity*,[15] entered schools with a missionary zeal. They challenged the established routines of grammar, précis and business English to emphasise the authenticity and spontaneity of children's own experiences and writing. The celebrated *Kes*[16] reflected the belief of many teachers that the intrinsic worth, merit and personality of children rarely engaged with schools that often seemed no more than cynical or unthinking outposts of 'the system'. Children were encouraged to express themselves in their own natural language. The movement found itself on trial at William Tyndale,[17] a *cause célèbre* used to discredit imaginative teaching of all kinds, although what was superficially at stake was the mismanagement of one primary school. 'Can they spell?' it was asked; a rhetorical question that had to be taken seriously. The idea that teachers might help children engage with literature and find a means of enrichment was altogether too subtle for the coarse debate of those days. 'Back to basics!' howled the popular press, themselves scarcely a model of articulate or balanced prose. Some teachers joined the chorus.

The political threat implicit in the Tyndale controversy and heightened by the Black Papers,[18] was elegantly appeased by the Bullock Report[19]. Bullock managed to evade the issue of 'standards' by offering an account of English in which 'skills' could be isolated and learned in step-by-step sequences; a 'language for life' became an elaborate, sophisticated drill, suitable material for a sergeant-instructor. For example, Bullock describes the '*intermediate skills* as the ability to handle sequences of letters, words and larger units of meaning. To acquire it the reader has to become familiar with the probability with which sequences occur'.[20] Bullock sketches for the patient reader a jigsaw of components.

Michael Marland, in *Language Across the Curriculum*,[21]

continued the retreat from 'English for maturity', responding to the new mood. He advises the teacher how to identify and remedy problems with language as they occur, in every subject of the curriculum. He recommends, for example, a 'spine' of learning skills for all subjects to be taught and reinforced by use; the composition of a glossary to be agreed and used by all staff; the adoption of a policy on the introduction of new words and concepts; the giving of a systematic training in non-narrative reading; and the teaching of spelling and punctuation.

A medical analogy suggests the limitations of this model of language teaching. Donald Gould[22] argues that the impact of the National Health Service on the health of the population at large has been very small indeed. A kidney machine or an appendix operation is of obvious benefit for the individual but overall health statistics do not seem much improved. The crucial factors influencing health are in fact environmental: cigarettes, lack of exercise, diet, social background, accidents, or exposure to chemicals should receive attention rather than individual organic 'malfunction'. Dr Gould points out that intensive-care units have only marginally lengthened the lives of coronary victims, and that for a man of fifty life expectancy has not been raised since the Crimean War. Health, and perhaps language too, is a social, cultural product inextricably entangled in 'the way we live now.' Literacy, like health, is more than the sum of its parts and treatments. It is embedded in the matrix of experiences shared by whole communities and socio-economic classes. Language is inseparable from experience and its development involves the whole person, not skills trained up like muscles on a bull-worker. A child's use (or misuse) of language contains his or her life's experience, not mistakes and oversights perpetrated with almost wilful carelessness.

Teachers must start with pupils and their accustomed language, setting aside the arcane world of text-books and a specialised, abstract vocabulary. Their aim should be to extend children's talk and writing through group work, proceeding from the particular to the general to enlarge knowledge and understanding together.

CHAPTER 5

Teaching methods

Most reform proposals are concerned with 'why' and 'what' questions, failing to appreciate that change can succeed only when an appropriate method has been worked out. David Hargreaves, for example, recommends 'an integrated course in community studies'[1] while the DES insists that:

> During the five secondary years, every pupil should study, on a worthwhile scale, history, geography, and under whatever guise (which may in some cases be history or geography), the principles underlying a free society and some basic economic awareness.[2]

Each of these statements assumes that certain types of desirable knowledge lead to particular ends. Hargreaves hopes for working-class enlightenment while the DES note expects the Humanities to underwrite liberal forms of society. Their confidence is similar to that of Fabians like Sidney and Beatrice Webb who believed that the collection and description of relevant facts would point towards the creation of municipal and state monopolies, their own favoured solution. A set of syllabuses listing topics to be covered is, however, an inadequate guide to the learning that takes place in a particular school. Subjects are changed by the mode of enquiry adopted, while exercises and activities leave a more permanent mark than 'the three field system' or 'volcanoes'.

Few schools have recognised how much understanding depends upon the form of a lesson, or how techniques involving active study and group interaction can enrich experience and learning. Teachers are mainly preoccupied with communicating knowledge, adopting an information-processing method inherited from grammar schools. An emphasis upon the progress of individuals towards ends prescribed for them in advance has prevented many, particularly in 'classroom subjects', from organising lessons like the basketball coach.[3]

Individualised learning

The extent to which schools rely upon factual teaching directed at passive, individual pupils is disguised by a crowded, sociable atmosphere. Inside the classroom, however, students are expected to be silent unless a question is asked. Permission to answer has to be obtained; no conferring is permitted. Written work must be prepared without help from neighbours; there is no worse offence than copying or collaborating. A test is set; desks are moved apart to prevent cheating; marks are awarded, praise and blame are distributed. Originality and silence are high virtues; talking or dialogue is prohibited unless the teacher is at the centre of it.

Events follow the crudest Victorian Sunday-school model according to an elementary stick-and-carrot psychology. It is a puritanical world in which no child would learn who might idle instead. Pleasure is supposed to be derived from success, or at least the avoidance of punishment, not from learning or curiosity. Understanding assumes a tabulated, sequential form, parallel to the career ladder that is extended as a mercenary inducement. Self-consciously progressive schools, anxious to promote the autonomy of their pupils and misunderstanding the problem, can make matters even worse. Children are occupied almost entirely by programmed worksheets so that the loneliness of private study is substituted for social activity of any kind.

The prevalence of individual methods can be gauged from

what happens even at primary level. In many infant and junior schools an alternative, social learning method seems to operate. Tables and chairs are arranged to suggest teams of five or six pupils engaged in a common endeavour. Creative work in Art and Craft appears a more natural vehicle for such an approach than secondary Mathematics or Foreign Languages. Disappointingly, these appearances are deceptive. Group work is often as accidental and incidental at this stage as it is later. Pupils sit in circles but their individual programmes are tightly structured to ensure their correct development. Activities follow one another in an insistent sequence based upon progress towards prescribed objectives. Children are seldom asked to work things out or plan their studies together or collaborate in an exercise.

Secondary schools continue the pattern. Children are organised to learn defined lists of facts or to master skills step by step. Experience is discounted as a route to understanding. The teacher or a book is perceived as an authoritative source of information; pupil interaction becomes a diversion from secure content that can be revised and tested.

The policy of teaching pupils as individuals derives from the belief that children's ability can be accurately measured and that the differences discovered are important in determining appropriate methods. The idea has proved unworkable in practice, as the use of bland stereotypes like 'bright' and 'less able' suggests. Instead of fine discrimination between individuals, teachers are left with categories as general as those of social class. No particular teaching methods have been invented for 'able' or 'dim' pupils; CSE and GCE examination questions, for example, often presume similar types of understanding and experience. 'Less able' pupils are expected to 'move more slowly' and to use a simpler vocabulary; teachers have not otherwise discovered means of varying their approach to match the 'ability level' of their pupils. Many schools nevertheless arrange finely tuned sets and streams as if ability and teaching can be adjusted to one another like cloth on a tailor's dummy. Strangely, teachers who are most anxious to persevere with banding or setting in the early years accept the much broader and often mixed CSE and GCE groups created by option choice.

Class sizes further frustrate those who wish to teach according to the differences between individuals. Pupils can expect only a few moments' attention in a lesson. Schools seek to resolve the problem by forming relatively homogeneous sets, but almost any selection of thirty pupils will contain a wide variety of distinctive learning needs. Some pupils will soon present themselves as 'bright' pacesetters while others will languish in despair at the bottom. It is a strange phenomenon that when a given population is divided and re-divided a normal distribution curve of performance reappears within each of the new groups. Even a cohort of students whose results over thirteen years or so have been sufficiently similar and remarkable to earn university places are subsequently likely to be awarded a full range of marks leading to good and bad degrees. By force of circumstances teachers frame assignments and methods to suit a vague, indefinable spectrum of ability.

There are doubts too about the validity and consistency of the test instruments used in many schools to establish sets. Some use primary school scores although each contributor may teach different topics or mark according to an uneven standard. Others apply 'whole year' examinations although different teachers have approached the material with varying skill and enthusiasm. Alternatively, sets are based upon teacher impressions of effort and aptitude. The technique of using results from one subject (e.g. English) to determine sets in another (e.g. History) is especially unsatisfactory.

Teachers are reluctant to recognise that it is impractical to identify individuals or groups for instruction according to an appropriate, differentiated method and are sometimes puzzled by the consequences of over-emphasising variations in pupil performance. Streaming can create undesirable social divisions and cause pupils to live up or down to a label. Schools are, in fact, most successful when providing shared, communal experiences and despite great ingenuity generally fail to meet special or individual needs. Classes constructed as a microcosm of the community are the most natural arrangement for a common school but meritocratic ideas have been so ingrained that comprehensives have been slow to adopt cooperative, group-learning methods. Mixed-ability teaching is a

relatively rare phenomenon. Teachers have missed the point
that although children vary in ability their common experience and responsibilities are of greater importance in planning
education.

The decision to work with undifferentiated groups rather
than isolated individuals is not motivated by a desire to
engineer equality or to restrict achievement. On the contrary,
once teachers come to plan learning as a social, interactive
process they may discover that individuals are extended more
effectively by shared experience than by isolated study of a
text. It is psychologically unsound to educate individuals
without reference to their peers and neighbours. As lessons are
at present organised, competition discourages the majority
and stimulates a few while peer group pressures work against
learning. Pupils who work hard are seen by their fellows as
engaged upon an alien exercise in self-improvement and most
students despise knowledge as well as their own efforts to
acquire it. The cooperative principle can be enlisted to create a
positive enjoyment of and enthusiasm for study as well as
practice for community politics.

Once a social, mixed-ability method is adopted, new
perspectives are opened and teachers are freed from the
mechanism of self-help schooling. Children can work
together, sharing both learning and achievement. Teachers
become organisers of structured activities, as much concerned
with talk, problem-solving and experiment as with private
writing. The group can become a legitimate focus of interest
and its potential can be mobilised as a resource in reconstruct-
ing events and simulating reality. Each student's value is
emphasised by the open and accessible form of the activities
now offered; swift judgements and preconceptions are less
possible.

Obstacles to group work

Many teachers are tentative about embarking upon a new
method, however attractive, for 'survival' considerations discussed above.[4] It is, after all, more difficult to manage, monitor and measure pupil activity than private reading or a lecture.

Wells's demonstration (see above, page 90) is straightforward compared with a typical circus of investigations conceived according to Nuffield principles.

Another source of hesitation is the lack of published resources for group use. Educational publishers, for sound commercial reasons, imitate the preoccupations of subject specialists, providing content and coverage in almost teacher-proof form. But for the pictures and plain prose no one would know most schoolbooks are designed to support lessons. The connotations of the term 'text-book', with hints of sermons and improving literature, are not encouraging. Note-taking is a natural activity arising from the available materials.

A further problem is the 'subject specialist' self-image developed since the demise of teaching certificates and secondary moderns. Teachers have a sense of their subject and value expertise; they hasten from local, informal experiences towards abstraction and formality. There is so much to be learned that no delay can be entertained, however rewarding. Children are taught to edit their vocabulary and language to accommodate traditions of scholarship; third-person prose is required for Science, set verbal formulae are needed everywhere. Sixth-form students worry that if they have not caught the correct sequence of words used by the book or teacher they may lose the idea. Teachers fear that if notebooks are not filled with coherent paragraphs, couched in acceptable terms, pupils will carry nothing with them from the lesson. What cannot be recorded and taken away is somehow less valid. It is as if what children learn is contained in their exercise books or examination scripts; teaching is planned like a fast food counter. Children chattering, even in a structured or organised manner, seem to risk ignorance; speech is a medium of exchange that cannot be coped with by existing concepts of 'book' learning that underpin preparation for examinations in most subjects. Teachers expect that parents and colleagues will interpret the orderliness of their classrooms and the neatness of pupils' notebooks as evidence of what has been taught; everyone is conditioned by similar traditions, learned by each generation at school.

The cruel deficiencies of present methods remain all the same. There are few planned opportunities for developing and extending ordinary, local language. Pupils have limited chances to use words with which they are proficient to explore ideas, concepts and content; instead they read or copy from blackboard and book, beginning and ending with the same finished article, a formal, professional, subject discourse. Fieldwork and experiments tend to be exceptions, not a starting point for all teaching. Ordinary observation rarely takes place because there is little to observe; how many essays on steam engines or cotton mills are based on more than a hazy notion of dirt and noise? Models and machines (even Technical Lego) are seldom used to illustrate ideas teachers expect children to learn from a description. Great issues of religion, economics, politics and culture are dealt with as if their connection with people were accidental. The events in books seem quite unlike life. Exploration, investigation, discussion, personal experience and experimentation play only a minor part in classrooms. Thought is supposed to travel in logical, empirical directions with deductions following one another with a growing momentum. Serendipity, dreaming, coincidence; elliptical or circular thinking; these are precluded by pace and discipline.

Pupils seldom plan their work or have a measure of responsibility for their own actions; they rarely take decisions or see the consequences of their moves within a child-centred timescale. This is perhaps surprising in a system designed to help individuals. Such a weakness within the individualist method illustrates the self-defeating character of isolation. Decisions cannot be taken about texts; either exercises are completed or they are not. A pupil sitting alone at a desk cannot accept responsibility for anything except action or inaction; prefects may supervise a staircase but their learning is by nature free of responsibilities after an initial decision to comply. Children do not plan essays about volcanoes or investigate the earth; instead they summarise or make notes as directed.

Most of these problems are caused by an unsatisfactory insight into child psychology. Children are not allowed to work together although cooperative social relations would enable them to do their best without stress or anxiety. Official lessons are mainly devoted to restricting the number of possible interactions between thirty people to a minimum. Talk comprises 'sheepdog' phrases in which the teacher directs, rebukes and rallies the class through a task, despite an unofficial hum of miscellaneous conversation irrelevant to the work in hand, serving rather as relief from it. Teachers talk to the class or individuals; pupils talk to teachers; official channels are narrow and restricting, as if an atmosphere of silent prayer were appropriate for good learning. The development of individuals, despite so much concern, is retarded because so few of the rich opportunities of the classroom and community have been exploited. Children need to share and direct one another's learning if they are to gain anything worthwhile from the subject presented. Nothing else matters as much as this single point; children must take part, they must work and talk together, and a lesson should not move on until pupils can express its main idea in their own words.

Schools Council and other projects

Like an ocean liner at sea the education system turns but slowly. Tiller and engine function well enough at their own pace in the direction first visualised by their builders but can seem defective in the hands of navigators with new charts.

As the social foundations of the common school are consolidated, however, there are encouraging signs of a developing 'comprehensive' teaching method upon which to build. Few teachers would deny that learning depends upon pupils thinking for themselves, upon opportunities for investigation and discovery. Curriculum development in a number of areas points towards an active, participatory mode. Teachers have responded eagerly to alternatives when these have been presented, so their commitment to archaic methods or their ability to adapt should not be inferred from present practice.

New methods in Geography, based on structures and models, flow through the Oxford Geography Project, Rex Walford's Longman Geography Games and the Schools Council's 'Geography for the Young School Leaver'. Woodwork teachers concerned with a tradition of craft skills are faintly embarrassed by the rapid spread of Craft, Design and

Technology, with its emphasis on problem-solving and an integrated approach. David Holbrook helped to show the significance of children's own speech and writing as a means of expression and discovery.[5] HMI stress oral and informal language in their own publications. The SMP has bewildered parents but shows that numbers are about relationships that can be explored and understood. Mechanical rules and unreflecting proofs appear less sensible in their light.

The curriculum work of the 1960s and 1970s, although not explicitly directed towards teaching methods, has led to a revision of long-standing assumptions. Each project has adopted, almost as an article of faith, the view that all children should work through concepts for themselves. None of the innovations has depended upon dividing pupils according to ability; the aim has been to involve all pupils in positive, thoughtful activity. Publishers have been unable to provide finely graded courses for each ability level (e.g. set 1, 2, etc.), leaving open the possibility that the attempt to educate by differences may not be justified.

The impact and repercussions of curriculum projects designed for comprehensive schools have been varied and difficult to define. Conventions and habits have proven remarkably resistant to change; project materials have been adapted and plagiarised, not always to be used as their authors intended. The Humanities Curriculum Project is often to be found in pristine plastic bags in obscure cupboards, its precepts remote from daily life and expressed without attention to teachers' needs. New ideas about what is involved in learning have been established nevertheless. This chapter's recommondations do not stand in utopian isolation. Teachers are well prepared to focus upon the process and activity of learning and how it is managed in the classroom but have still to escape the boa-grip of self-help individualism. By themselves these developments can lead to better teaching; exciting possibilities have been opened for many teachers. To be fully effective, however, improvements in method need to be related to other group and community issues and to be applied to the whole curriculum.

Pupils and their neighbourhoods have to be rescued from the condescension of the self-improvers so that learning may rediscover its social and sociable origins. Teaching methods, however ingenious, will have a mainly technical impact until they form part of a group approach. The methodological premise of individualism will not be altered merely by adding social and community studies to the curriculum. The community can be studied just as all the other 'academic' subjects are studied. Sociology in itself is not enough. New methods developed from encouraging features of current practice are enabling teachers to adapt their work by steady degrees, gaining in confidence and understanding of their role as leaders of groups.

Planning lessons

Classrooms crowded with pupils and furniture demand management skills of a high order for constructive learning to take place. The teacher's ability to project and embody a plan of events creates the security within which pupils can think and talk through problems, arrive at decisions or take action. Territory, movement, progression from one stage to another, timing and sequencing all depend upon control. With the present level of resources it is unrealistic to expect pupils in the early years of secondary school to manage their own learning from beginning to end. If pupils are left not knowing what is expected or what it is they are supposed to plan, disorder will swiftly follow. Apparently independent project and topic work can turn out to be no more than copying from books, with minimal interaction between pupils. Effective relationships depend upon the quality of leadership available. Events need to be made to flow; fruitless discussion needs to be redirected, inattention to be dealt with.

Group exercises depend for success upon a number of strategic decisions. Teachers should plan to cover very much less ground than before. Time needs to be allowed for groups to be formed and organised for work; discussion and participation are not a speedy business. Topics should be arranged to ensure that important concepts are examined in a sensible order, but a narrowly sequential approach will inhibit progress. When a class plays a passive role the flow of subject matter is more easily controlled; learning in and with a group is likely, by contrast, to be episodic and tangential. Active involvement can be frustrated by too tight or too detailed control; pace is necessary to sustain interest. Fewer topics should be studied to allow more time for each. Case studies enable students to develop ideas in a definite context, moving from the specific and particular to general reflections. One farm and its problems may prove more illuminating than a survey of European agriculture. Authentic, detailed source material can be arranged to support a special study where attention can be more easily focused. Narrative or descriptive techniques can freeze concepts into a single frame of reference or context, discouraging pupils from making connections or comparisons. Isolated facts tend to make sense only in the original sequence.

Children's own role in lessons should be emphasised. Every pupil can contribute if closed exercises and questions are avoided. Pupils should be free to develop and explore ideas, able to follow unexpected lines of association or enquiry. Responses and activity, for example, can be restricted unconsciously by questions or instructions designed to establish factual sequences or test memory. A lesson should provide an initial stimulus leading to group activity and response; the stimulus needs to be devised so that students can speculate and debate before arriving at a solution or conclusion. There should be ample opportunity for the response to be elaborated, planned and extended.

Exercises should permit a great variety of interactions within and between groups of varying size and composition so that pupils can experience and manage different social contexts. Clear instructions and a careful structure are necessary for genuinely self-directed work; planning and organising are possible only if the goals are plain and the means available. Where possible (but especially in the Humanities) the pupils themselves should be used to reconstruct or simulate the cardinal features of a subject. Pupil talk, a medium for internalising ideas, can find scope only when transactions are extended beyond the teacher–taught relationship.

These suggestions need to be applied systematically if schools are to lose their meritocratic, individualist obsessions.

Group work is not, however, an exclusive doctrine, sufficient in itself to change the pattern of education, nor should lectures, demonstrations, private study, reading and tests of factual recall be discounted in future. Variety of approach is refreshing and stimulating for teachers and pupils alike and it is the dreary sameness of lessons as they are that has prompted the demand for change. The effort to recover the social dimension of language and learning should not obscure the reality that a method's effectiveness depends upon its fitness for the intention or purpose of the moment. Applying these principles in practical exercises requires considerable ingenuity as well as energy and resources. Teams of teachers, teacher centres, university departments of education, colleges of higher education and publishers need to work together to generate a bank of materials to help implement a group approach. An individual teacher is as vulnerable as an individual pupil.

The essential technique of groupwork is straightforward, nevertheless. A role or task should be created for each member to perform, enabling children to feel that they share in the ownership of some real, immediate problem or issue. Subject matter should not be presented as an abstract language game. Comprehension tests, or other questions requiring inferences to be made from a text, provide no point of access for students or any opportunity to identify with the problem or its solution. Questions should be phrased as if addressed to a participant; pupils should be enabled to feel a common interest in what is happening so that a mistaken decision *affects them*.

Questions

Detached observation is possible later but in the early stages children respond better if they can experience what has happened or might happen from the inside. Questions beginning 'What would you do if . . . ?' 'Which would you choose . . . ?' represent an open-ended invitation; it is closed or withdrawn by asking 'What does the author mean in line four?' It is essential to stop asking children to remember, find out, learn; the shopping list approach implied in the question

'What do you know about Canada?' is wholly unsuitable for this purpose. Children should see the reality of what is happening and feel that it could happen to them. No one should search through books to extrapolate words, sentences or paragraphs that may fill the blanks (or prompt-spaces) left by the teacher, as happens with many apparently child-centred, independent work programmes. Identification creates a bridge between the pupil's experience and the concepts to be learned. It provides a fixed point from which the group can explore possible answers, using whatever language is mutually understood, before collectively deciding what is most appropriate.

Students have to think outwards from a moment of empathy, working in pairs, threes or fours according to the structure of the exercise. What each member of the group has to contribute or do should be explicit. Teachers should explain the structure of activities; the verbal complexity of any rules or instructions is not a necessary indication of the level of difficulty of an exercise. Group members themselves determine the level or quality of their response; the assignment is a suggestive framework or starting point for responses, not a self-contained and self-defining question. Cookery recipes are a helpful analogy: a good formula does not in itself bake a satisfactory cake but within the limits laid down by a chef the materials and recipe provide a powerful basis for learning culinary skills.

Further progress or development should depend on the learner's own activity; the pupil prepares and steps forward, fresh information coming in the form of answers to enquiries or through the test of an idea. It is not necessary to produce an elaborate structure provided the technique of questioning required is understood. For example:

(a) Make a nail-box according to the following measurements and instructions
    BECOMES
(b) Design a bridge with the maximum span possible using eight pieces of wood

(c) Describe the steps by which Britain found itself at war with Germany in 1939

BECOMES
(d) If you were Winston Churchill how would you respond to Hitler's peace offer and why?

(e) Copy the sketch of a locust into your book
BECOMES
(f) What suggestions have you for controlling locusts?

(g) In what conditions does barley grow best?
BECOMES
(h) If you were the farmer where would you plant barley?

Questions converted according to the above prescriptions lead to obvious and natural activity. Additional materials, for example photographs, maps, evidence, lists of facts and options, and equipment, give a basis for working out solutions.

The teacher should divide the class into small groups according to the nature of the task, stating in advance when the next phase of an exercise is due. Tasks or roles can be allocated to each group (e.g. 'employers' in a simulation of industrial relations) or to individuals within a group; it may be that two or three pupils will be asked to investigate a problem or solve a puzzle; they may have to develop a strategy for preventing vandalism or siting an oil well. Open-endedness should not become an excuse for providing insufficient information (e.g. 'Imagine that . . .') or inadequate material. Basic information about the life cycle and habits of the locust is necessary and should be to hand.

The approach recommended here is pupil-centred in the sense that the student has the initiative and the teacher has always to think in terms of pupil activity. Teaching remains recognisably orthodox: schemes are devised and organised by teachers to ensure that work is focused on topics and concepts deemed important by the school. Pupils should not take curriculum decisions; in this respect teachers are natural and inevitable leaders, planning students' growth. Yet children must be free to work together within a given structure, taking fundamental learning decisions for themselves. Materials and questions set limits and restrict the range of answers, but the stress is upon the inventiveness of the pupils. Their ability to manage themselves, and their group's ability to design and implement ideas, will be as important as the concepts offered for consideration. Activity and response are as influential as the structure of the exercise and its content in contributing to understanding.

An effective safeguard is to ensure that exercises contain a point where decisions or action leading to resolution are required. How will the group invest its capital? In which direction should the army attack? What tests are necessary to identify a compound? Where should the drilling platform be located? Which option should be selected? Who should pay tax or have the vote? The fruits of speculation and discussion have then to be applied and tested against reality. The false distinction between theory and practice noted earlier is in this way dissolved. Theoretical ideas and practical skills are integrated by the process of group decision-making. A theory cannot be developed without research, observation and experiment (which themselves depend on activity) and will be rejected unless it has some application or relevance. Children will learn what they need to solve a problem or design a solution (using the available data) untroubled by a specialist edifice of theory and knowledge. Concepts and ideas are given a tangible reality by the need to choose, to select, to apply, to decide or act, and are assimilated through the social experience of group learning. An exercise's framework should allow for experimentation with alternative solutions, testing a variety of more or less satisfactory answers to destruction. The ingredients of an activity need to be laid out clearly with a variety of consequences planned in. Answers should not come to mind too readily; other, equally possible choices should commend themselves.

Relationships

There is more to the reform of teaching methods than an emphasis on thinking skills or cognitive processes. The relationship between students should not be left to the accidents of the 'hidden curriculum'. Teamwork and cooperation matter most in the classroom; individualised learning must be reduced as part of a strategic plan to promote effective lessons. Children can contribute in groups where they may flounder as

individuals; the threat of a direct question, and the embarrass-
ment of the public and almost theatrical pupil–teacher dialogue, is removed. There will be an infinitely more complex
web of relations and many more opportunities for youngsters
to join in. Pupils will lose some of their inhibitions and
reservations; their ideas will be expressed in their own terms
and language in a series of trials with friends before being
tested against reality. The fear of failure will be diminished and
the opportunity to succeed broadened. The trial-and-error of
regular experiment by teams of students working together
ensures that new methods are not lost in their own cleverness.

Group activity should lead to a clear outcome or specific
conclusion but teachers ought to resist the temptation to round
off lessons with written records. Drama, model-making or
conversation do not need to be legitimised by essays; children
learn what they experience. It is not the answers children
produce or even the solutions offered that matter but the
exercise of their faculties in a host of media (dramatic, numerical, verbal, musical, material).

Whatever the activity (from performing and making to
calculating and writing), pupils are exercising an aesthetic
judgement that is the mainspring of human activity. Pupils
should be encouraged to attempt a range of responses; the
result of their work need not be identifiably their own on every
occasion. On the other hand, collaboration does not necessarily involve the loss of individual authorship. Teachers will
need to respond to children's work sensitively and thought-
fully, judging the needs of individuals and groups for further
development on the evidence before them.

Group work is a means to make better lessons, not an
ideology. Individuals can still excel and should be rewarded by
praise. Pupils know how they stand in relation to others,
however teachers seek to disguise an unpleasant truth. There is
no virtue in an Alice-in-Wonderland fantasy world in which
'all have won and all shall have prizes'. Youngsters are not
encouraged if their work is unrecognised or, alternatively, is
praised or cursed indiscriminately. Pupils are in no sense equal;
differences are real enough even if they are not helpful as a
guide in setting work. Positive comment and positive criticism should be offered; teachers should not abstain from

judgement or impressions. Provided invidious or unnecessari-
ly discouraging remarks can be avoided, merit may still
delight. Teachers cannot easily play a neutral part and the
value of such neutrality is uncertain. But despite delight the
emphasis with group work is upon the quality of response
made by every pupil, not upon individual achievement. Too
much has been made in the past of the exceptional, and too
little of the ordinary but effective.

Success achieved by individuals in isolation from their
communities and peers by a process of specialisation and
separation is artificial because it reinforces a tendency to
discount as citizens those who show no early symptoms of
expertise. A radical reform of teaching methods is therefore an
essential part of the strategy to rediscover talent and merit in
the common school.

CHAPTER 6

Assessment and examinations

Public examinations highlight the mismatch between a common school and a divisive system of education designed to advance individuals. Teachers and parents are committed to competitive assessment in specialist subjects, without apparently recognising the implications of tests that reward only a successful few. A school leaver can obtain twelve possible grades in each subject (i.e. GCE A–U; CSE 1–U) but educationists and employers really value only the top fifth of these. Examination Boards expect an average pupil to score 20 per cent on a typical paper and to be placed in the bottom two grades: a dismal, predetermined outcome for 15,000 hours in school. The attempt to discriminate between 'able' and 'less able' candidates that this represents is incompatible with the widespread desire to motivate and reward a majority of students.

Effective learning cannot be supported and reinforced by assessment methods based on horse-race principles. The general public studies the published results of this narrowly focused exercise before pronouncing judgement on the quality of a school, or upon state education in general, without understanding that statistics, rather than any intrinsic educational fact, are responsible for the profile of ability reflected in grades and certificates.

It is fashionable to complain of public examinations, blaming them for the often depressing attitudes and methods adopted during the last five terms of compulsory schooling. GCE and CSE are not an alien imposition, however, but an essential feature of a meritocratic, individualist philosophy of education. Teachers play a central part in the system as examiners, markers and moderators, and papers echo the style and content of most lessons. Schools are organised to meet the needs of a relatively small number of 'bright' students because they have not developed an alernative to the 'academic' and 'practical' framework discussed above, not as a result of pressure from universities or GCE Boards. Universities play a subtle and complex role; a great deal of lifeless teaching stems from the desire of graduates to communicate 'their' subject without considering how children learn, not from direct pressure on syllabuses and methods. At worst, public examinations serve to reinforce and perhaps codify the selective, discriminating, literary tendencies already at work.

The limits of assessment

These difficulties are not clear to clients who expect scores and marks to provide simple answers to straightforward questions. Parents want to know how their children compare with others, or which local school is best. Employers and politicians fear that standards have fallen since some hypothetical moment in the past. Students, trained to expect a trade-off between school work and later employment, seek a definitive grade. Public examinations represent the only attempt to satisfy this demand for facts, an isolated effort at an objective assessment after years of vague, tentative progress. As a result examinations have become increasingly important, inflated out of all proportion to their real contribution to helping children learn. They have become the focus of deep-seated hopes and anxieties, a sacred ritual of education. Teachers, tempted by doubt, are inclined to remember that they owe their position to almost uninterrupted success at competitive examinations.

GCE and CSE have inevitably disappointed these exaggerated expectations, providing deeply unsatisfactory answers to questions about standards or learning. Public examinations have a doubtful statistical base (a margin of error of 20 per cent is sufficient to misplace an average 'C' pupil in grade A or E) and measure students against one another, not by educational objectives. Papers are changed each year but questions are not standardised. Comparisons between one year and another therefore mean very little, traditions in different subjects and Boards influencing the percentage in each grade more than variations in the quality of candidate. Mark schemes and examiners' meetings reduce but do not eliminate the subjective response, particularly to essays, which are still a staple form of assessment. No one really knows what essays show about their authors; Boards aim simply to rank candidates by comparing one hurriedly composed sample with another. Tests that are more objective, requiring less complex pupil behaviour, tend to be reliable but are less educationally valid. If the paper records only shaded boxes or factual statements scant justice can be done to the thought processes involved.

Results emerging from such a doubtful procedure are unsatisfactory as a source of knowledge about pupils or schools and there is little point in aggregating them in the hope of detecting national trends or comparisons between Boards, LEAs, schools or historical periods. The powerful correlation established between parental occupation and individual examination results suggests that socio-economic class is a more influential variable than any other. At seemingly comparable schools, significant differences in results can be explained by entry policy. Schools control the number of candidates entered, the number of Boards, the mode of examination, the syllabuses followed, the number of subjects taken by each pupil and the level (i.e. GCE, CSE or double-entry) of entry. This is sufficient to complicate the business of interpreting either absolute numbers or percentages to the point at which sane observers conclude that the enterprise is not worthwhile.

If examinations cannot provide useful information about standards or the quality of education, do they help pupils, employers or teachers? After all, 'getting a better job' is the prime reason pupils cite for coming to school at all. Neither GCE nor CSE create jobs; their function is purely selective and distributive. Examination Boards cannot increase or even influence the number or the nature of employment opportunities. If pupils are especially diligent or teachers particularly skilful the effect is to transfer 'life chances', not to enlarge them. For example, the relatively weak economy of the north of England or lowland Scotland is stubbornly resistant to high quality school leavers or excellent schools.

GCE grades A–C and CSE grade 1 do function as a viable hurdle for higher and further education and the professions; they ensure an open competition of sorts for young people whose family circumstances predispose them to compete. School reports and interviews might yield a similar clerical, administrative and managerial population but examinations do provide an efficient benchmark for screening and selecting children, even if the criteria are unstated and the courses followed are irrelevant to future employment destinations. This benefit is barely sufficient to offset the negative consequences for the most successful pupils. They are taught to view learning as that which is necessary to win certificates, to become expert in hurried handwriting and at memorising points to which no future reference will be made. The shape and pattern of the last two years at school are built around an examination calendar with 'mocks', test papers, revision and practice questions occupying considerable time. Curiosity and spontaneity are driven from the field. For the final months all that remains is competition.

The narrowing effect is comparable to that once exercised by the eleven–plus on primary schools. Less than 10 per cent of the secondary population can gain from these arrangements. The remainder obtain employment or a Youth Training Scheme place before results become available in August; for all the alleged mistrust of schools, employers are happy to recruit on the basis of estimated grades, references and interviews. Some have their own selection boards. Other certificates and grades (except perhaps for Royal Society of Arts or City and Guilds qualifications directly relevant to a vocation) have almost no value. It is often better not to have tried at all than to have worked hard for the little-understood or -valued CSE grades 3–5. A diploma in 'Lifeskills' can seem evidence of difficulties with basic spelling and arithmetic, signifying the absence of precisely the skills supposedly certified. In the vocational market place, value is attached only to scarcity. The results earned by most candidates indicate nothing more than an average or less than average placing in a rank order vaguely connected with a subject of study. The competitors have entered a race with a large field and few prizes.

Teachers are sensitive and aware enough to share the disappointment of their pupils and to lack conviction about examinations that have become the focus of school life. Criticism would be sharper still were teachers not conditioned to think of many students as natural failures, nearly incapable of objectively measurable learning. The lifeless, slow atmosphere of an average CSE set can be interpreted as a reflection of the students themselves rather than a result of the organisation and content of lessons. A critical reappraisal of teaching policies is discouraged by the emphasis on examinations, and many teachers are inclined to blame the system for deficiencies rooted in their own assumptions and practice.

Internal school assessments, for example, are norm-referenced, based on a comparison between students of similar age rather than measuring progress towards educational targets. Aims and objectives sometimes preface syllabuses and schemes of work; they are seldom specifically assessed unless an element of practical or oral activity forms part of the course. This lack of definition and clarity is reflected in test questions. Items intended to measure aspects of understanding in Geography may instead test competence in arithmetic and language. Unlike their public equivalent, school assessments, from the homework assignment to the test paper, can be crudely marked and ranked on the basis of subjective, impressionistic judgements. Mark ranges are narrowed by the absence of criteria or mark schemes and few staff know how to standardise marks. Standardised tests are used only for specialised, diagnostic purposes. In terms of content, school assessments closely resemble public examinations. There is the same reliance on essays and factual recall; continuous assessment, oral and practical tests are perhaps a more common feature of *external* examinations. Few schools maintain careful records of what pupils can do or correlate performances in different subject areas. There is no evidence that teachers would do things differently if they were more directly responsible for CSE or GCE. Indeed, CSE mode III papers (for which teachers write the syllabus and questions) often duplicate mode I syllabuses offered by regional Boards and one another.

Plans for reform

Ambiguous and ambivalent discontent from miscellaneous sources has, just the same, proved a powerful motor for change, spawning innumerable initiatives for reform. Yet few of these have recognised the central dilemma. If the examination system is used to select a few individuals for high status, limited opportunities in further education and some parts of the labour market, it cannot also serve broadly based educational objectives. Reformers have tackled issues of content and method, hoping to influence teaching; they have challenged the technical basis of existing assessments; they propose innovations such as profiles and a common examination related to criteria at sixteen-plus. There is certainty about the need to change but an underlying confusion about both means and ends. Is the proposed General Certificate of Secondary Education (GCSE) mainly a clarification of administrative arrangements or a radical departure in the measurement of educational outcomes? Is it intended to increase the pressure within the confines of existing disciplines or to make examinations more rewarding for the majority? Aims such as these are not necessarily incompatible but it is doubtful whether examinations that remain specialised in subject matter and discriminate sharply between candidates can also have a comprehensive and inclusive practical effect.

The most prolonged debate concerns the supposed over-specialised character of work in the sixth form for Advanced level. For some twenty years ideas have been developed to broaden the curriculum of the most able 7 or 8 per cent who choose to remain at school; courses for those with below 'A' level potential have received attention only since the advent of the MSC. Universities worried about allegedly 'illiterate' undergraduates briefly demanded a pass in the 'Use of English' in addition to 'O' level English Language. The foolish prejudice that discounted the most successful students as 'illiterate' or lacking in 'general' education prompted the General Studies movement (including a Schools Council project and new examinations in subject matter deemed general). Dissatisfied, the Schools Council recommended more radical action, seeking to replace GCE Advanced level with 'Normal' and 'Further' papers, threatening a fabulous burden of work for students to ensure their expertise in Darwin as well as in Shakespeare. There were not many things about which a 'bright' seventeen-year-old might not be examined. Special papers, soon to be replaced by a further variation on the principle of excessive study, set out to foster the peculiar hybrid of a general knowledge of a specialised subject.

Why was such an energetic investigation of specialisation confined to the two-year sixth form? Sixth-formers are not educated at the last hurdle; specialised, literary content is a dominant feature of most secondary and even some primary education. The notion that students with eight or nine GCE 'O' levels lacked 'general' knowledge did not lead to a wider critique of the curriculum. It was assumed that additional or supplementary courses would be sufficient. Teachers were unwilling to surrender a millimetre of the Science syllabus for an inch of grammar or a verse of poetry. It was easier to complain of the 'illiteracy' of clever scientists than to recognise the discouraging effect of dull, narrow teaching upon most students on 'O' and 'A' level courses. The proposed improvements in fact entailed more reading and writing; a greater volume of work of a similar nature. Personal projects, oral and practical activity, group investigations and fieldwork were suggested as *extensions*, not as alternatives, to essays and lectures.

The most discouraging feature of this episode is, however, that debate and research should have yielded nothing of practical value, exerting almost no influence on schools, where Advanced work continues more or less as it has always done. It is a tale sufficient to inspire caution in the most impetuous reformer.

The proposed common examination at sixteen-plus has a parallel history of gestation and miscarriage only narrowly escaping a similar fate. GCSE will be offered for the first time in 1986. In this case reform is the climax of a long search for a system of examining suitable for comprehensive schools.

Present dual arrangements with innumerable Boards offering thousands of syllabuses are an administrative nightmare, consuming every available hour between March and June, at a cost in excess of the total capitation set aside by local authorities for fifth-form students. Each school, and often each department within a school, selects a GCE Board and syllabus that it believes to be favourable. GCE is seldom compatible with the regional CSE board's version of the same subject. Pupils have to be divided into GCE/CSE sheep or goats and the examination timetable can be so complex that individual candidates with peculiar combinations of papers sometimes have to have a personal invigilator, who follows them even into the bathroom to safeguard the secrecy of questions.

The number of pupils entered for examination varies greatly from school to school. One teacher may enter all pupils, hoping perhaps to dilute the standard required for each grade; another may enter only the able to protect a personal pass rate. From the pupil's point of view there is no coherence or shape about the resulting pattern of subjects taken; numbers might just as well be called in a bingo parlour. School option schemes are designed primarily to give pupils a wide range of subject choices and the maximum number of tickets in the examination lottery. Examination results are insufficiently reliable to give teachers confidence in making entry decisions; subject by subject and pupil by pupil, the variation is enough to make nonsense of the 'borderline' cases over which staff agonise. The result is a 'black economy' with many pupils entered for the same subject several times over, with different boards or at both CSE and GCE. The status of CSE is doubtful, which compounds the perplexity of teachers and candidates.

There is an obvious need for a single, common examination to simplify and clarify the system and resolve some of these complex issues. Unfortunately some aspects of GCSE could in practice exacerbate the damaging features of existing public examinations. The preparation of national criteria for syllabuses could, for example, narrow and standardise the curriculum without achieving a coherent definition. An elaborate web of papers linked to grade ceilings to cater for a wide ability range may prove as confusing and difficult to administer as the dual system. The plan to measure performance against precise educational criteria rather than by comparison with other candidates may prove a time-bomb beneath the whole enterprise. As shown above, it is doubtful whether educational objectives can be defined with adequate precision or whether test items can be sufficiently consistent or specific for this purpose. It is as difficult to assess objectives as to describe them unambiguously. The proposal to award a distinction for high grades on a group of subjects may mean that papers remain far too difficult for most candidates and discourage pupils and teachers alike. This is less than surprising because GCSE is not intended to alter the discriminating, selective, competitive features of present examinations.

Another type of reform proposal concerns assessment methods. There is continuing discontent with the narrowness of traditional examinations and their emphasis on factual recall and a journalistic facility with essays. Some would like to see assessment probe further into a candidate's capabilities; others seek to influence teaching through questions based more on process than content, testing for example oral and practical skills or the ability to think as well as regurgitate. Suggestions of this kind stem from unhappiness with existing arrangements rather than a considered view of the difficulties of implementing change. When teachers had something approaching a free hand in the drafting of examination papers there were few departures from standard forms of assessment. Projects were the only important innovation but these often proved to be little more than an exercise in neat handwriting and attractive presentation. Continuous assessment and the administration of school-based examinations have proved too time-consuming for most staff.

The value of active and oral methods is often stressed by those outside the schools, perhaps unaware of the difficulties caused by unavoidable practical testing in Languages, Science, Art and Craft. Lessons are disrupted for everyone else as two or three teachers in each of the subjects affected are withdrawn from the timetable to conduct individual assessments. It may be desirable for each pupil to engage in experiments and discussions conducted on a tutorial basis but this can be contrived only by increasing the resources devoted to examinations. There is something false about assessments that differ in character from the teaching offered. Individual assessment in spoken English is a strange end to a course conducted in sets of thirty.

Experiments with records of personal achievement seem on the surface the most promising of recent initiatives. Profiles seek a profound change in the method of defining and evaluating pupil performance, aiming to include many more skills and attributes than previously assessed. This is an ambitious thrust into uncharted waters with aims at variance with those of GCSE. Without an adequate definition or accurate measurement of the qualities of character and achievements recorded in the profile, it cannot hope to be an objective alternative to competitive examinations. The value of a profile dossier in the same market place as a GCSE group distinction is in any case doubtful. Records of 'personal achievement' could become time-consuming, inflated school reports, without much significance for teaching or learning plainly geared for GCSE. Pupils derive satisfaction and confidence from a success that is recognised on its own terms, not from contrived consolation prizes. GCSE is the statement of intent that will shape or fail to shape schools in the years ahead.

The pursuit of standards

Despite all experience, people still expect examinations to establish certain merit and definite standards, as if these were absolute properties to be discovered by scientific investigation. As seen above, many teachers and parents believe in 'bright' or 'intelligent' children whose learning can be precisely measured against objective criteria and whose general ability can be stated in terms of examination results. There is a deep reluctance to recognise that all judgements are subject to wide margins of error and relate only to a particular question or context. Examination Boards have no such pretensions, aiming only to rank candidates on the basis of answers to questions. No one attaches any particular meaning to the answers, questions or grades; all that is required of a paper is a reasonable coverage of syllabus content. Chief examiners do not redefine knowledge or education but process the scripts offered with considerable sophistication. It may be that this is the fairest, most economical compromise between learning and screening.

People interested in merit and standards as a matter of principle have challenged norm-referencing techniques, believing that a particular grade should have a consistent meaning year by year and that pupils should be judged by their absolute ability, not by comparison with others. Authors of the Black Papers have been especially worried by the fact that the standard, norm-referenced test is determined by the number and quality of candidates as much as by educational attainment. The idea of fixed grades referring to particular achievements, rather than a ranking established by statistical sleight of hand, has a wide appeal to teachers disillusioned by the arbitrary results of public examinations. The development of graded tests in Mathematics and Languages[1] has encouraged the belief that competencies can be precisely defined and tested, leading to improvements in teaching and motivation.

This experience is encouraging, but objective criterion-related tests can achieve greater validity and reliability only by reducing their subject to its most elementary and simple forms. Instrumental examinations are not Music; enquiring about a cup of coffee in a restaurant is not speaking French. Graded test items in the Humanities, or in aesthetic and creative subjects, would not be acceptable evidence of general understanding. There is no difficulty in defining or testing 'the ability to use a chisel'. More complex operations, by contrast, depend upon an interaction of skills each of which is difficult to describe. Who can be sure what is involved in 'designing a bridge'?

Should it prove possible to establish satisfactory, objective, criterion-related tests for clusters of mental activities, there is a further problem. Desmond Nuttall has shown that there is no satisfactory statistical instrument for guaranteeing the stability and reliability of results over time. Professor Nuttall's demolition of the Rasch model,[2] of which much was hoped, demonstrates that standards cannot exist independently of the expectations, subjective judgements and values of the examiner, who has a happy knack of getting what is expected, including the appropriate howlers. Tests inevitably shape and limit pupils' responses and have their own unpredictable and unintended bias that confuses the interpretation of the scores obtained. Oral or practical tests, for example, have a different effect from those confined to pencil and paper; how can an examiner be sure of not marking the fruit of a misunderstanding stemming from the phrasing of the question? Items are suspect if a child could obtain higher marks with a slight prompt or the opportunity to express ideas orally.

Criterion-referencing gives the false impression that the subjective and arbitrary quality of all public examinations can be escaped. APU researchers, for example, conduct extensive pre-tests of items to ensure that questions are reasonable. The benchmark for a criterion is therefore arrived at by norm-referencing. Without the Rasch model or a similar statistical device even this technique is an unsatisfactory basis for objective judgements. Teachers and educationists constantly make new judgements and ask new, or at least different, questions. The anxious parent's question is, in the end, the one that counts: 'How many others in your class got grade 2?' Grade 2 cannot offer a more subtle insight into the processes of human learning.

Underlying all these attempts at reform is the major cause of their failure. Employers, parents, teachers and the most articulate students, despite the reservations outlined above, are committed to the principles of discrimination and specialisation. An examination which does not satisfactorily discriminate between candidates, emphasising their differences, will not command public confidence. Examinations are expected to define and confirm high-status knowledge and respectable subjects, to be pure and proper, fulfilling a profound social as well as scholarly function. It will take an act of faith and political imagination to transcend these convictions and free learning in the schools from the burden of social prejudice. Education is unlikely to achieve enhanced participation and a measure of satisfaction for everyone until reformers recognise the limitations of assessment and the true potential of average children.

Assessment aims

The temptation to recommend the abolition of examinations that have become so external to the process of learning and so discouraging in their general effect is therefore very great. The difficulty is that without public assessment things might be even worse. Places in employment and higher education would remain limited and might be filled by less open and less fair means. Public confidence would be reduced and teachers might not adjust easily to the removal of external checks. Independent schools would enjoy a further improvement in their standing and would probably devise an alternative validation of their own, a 'Public School Certificate', perhaps. Some new system, possibly less pleasant than present arrangements, would be needed to measure what schools were doing. The sudden disappearance of public examinations without accompanying changes in expectations and teaching might not lead to better education. Deprived of the security of GCE and CSE, teachers might cling the more stubbornly to established practice. Many primary teachers, following a period of uncertainty in the aftermath of the eleven-plus, are anxious to emphasise 'the basics' in which primitive virtue is seen to reside. The primary precedent suggests that good practice stems from the professional confidence and planning of teachers, not the presence or absence of a free-standing external test.

It is surely more sensible to redress the balance in the debate, re-emphasising the positive function of assessment and insisting that examinations at all levels support teachers in their search for involvement and learning for all. As teaching methods develop assessment procedures should move in the same direction, seeking to reflect and reinforce the principles of active, open, cooperative learning. A flexible system could contribute to a profound and necessary change in teachers' beliefs and methods. Powerful tools should not be discarded simply because they are often abused. We should seek instead an effective, valid, national examination to help teachers and parents recognise the process of learning and understand their children. A decision to abandon racing will convince no one of the benefits of cooperation. Progress towards a more constructive assessment pattern depends, however, on changing critical features of existing provision.

The prime purpose of tests and questions is to define and organise material so that pupils and teachers can visualise the territory before them. A series of targets should be set to help youngsters achieve satisfaction and increasing confidence as they advance, perceiving more of the whole. Pupils need to be encouraged to extend themselves by pride in present success and the possibility of future attainment. Pleasure comes from tangible mastery reached within a reasonable timespan, not the repetition of a process or endeavour that does not lead to recognisable results. If a child learning cricket had to spend five years trying out bat and gloves before taking part in a match, there would be few attenders at after-school practices. This obvious psychological point too easily leads teachers into a crude stick-and-carrot approach. Children will compete for stars, praise, prizes or even house points but will not believe in their own success unless it is measurable against a definite yardstick. The chief incentive and enjoyment are derived from knowing or doing something previously mysterious. Students' knowledge of their own progress contributes more to self-esteem than do badges or certificates. Graded tests work because teaching for each level is organised around specific, attainable objectives with which children can identify. A certificate is a record of a trial, not the achievement itself. Learning must be valued and recognised for its own sake.

Test items must be interconnected with the work of teachers so that learning is monitored and assisted. A closer relationship between teaching, learning and assessment is necessary if examinations are to contribute towards improving education, rather than performing a mystic rite when school is over. Some of the negative impact of examinations upon teaching techniques and pupils' self-image might be reduced if mark ranges were limited and discrimination were less fine. Existing 'market' needs could be met with very few grades; employers and teachers share a common, very broad approach to selection and do not really need the dozen or so categories provided by the Examination Boards.

Examples of test items

Substantial progress is unlikely to be made in escaping the assessment dilemma until the teaching methods described in Chapter 5 are reflected in examination questions and test items. The examples[3] below show how classroom exercises can be used to evaluate or measure understanding. These illustrate how exercises supported by parallel assessment can help pupils develop and express a broad understanding of concepts previously considered beyond their reach.

Each item is open-ended. There are no right answers but degrees of reasonableness. Candidates are not expected to produce a full answer from their heads in response to a brief question; memorised facts are of marginal value. The test itself suggests ideas and provides the material for an answer. No pupil need be unprepared for a particular line of questioning. The emphasis is upon response and activity.

Problems are in an accessible format. Where possible maps, diagrams, checklists and a variety of prompts are included. Despite these efforts the questions remain of the pencil-and-paper type. Pupils who write standard English will have a considerable advantage. The cost of introducing oral and practical tests for all subjects and the additional burden for teachers imposed by continuous assessment mean that these alternatives are likely to be used sparingly. There is ample evidence that if children have the opportunity to apply concepts in a familiar, practical context their performance is much enhanced, a point in favour of improved pupil–teacher ratios and increased resources, although what can be done within existing limits should not be underestimated.

Each example is concerned with thinking *about* History, not with abstract thinking skills. Process and content are considered together, as they are in the teaching methods discussed above. No attempt is made to measure 'empathy', 'imagination' or 'analysis'; all require a full engagement with the human and material issues raised by the content. Skills can be described singly, but who can say what thought unfolds as children potter in the shadow of past events?

Although these items can be employed for testing individuals their use encourages small group discussion and co-operative working. These examples depend upon a pupil's familiarity with debate and dialogue; on an ability to organise and synthesise different points of view. The form of such assessment is individual but competitive learning is no longer the centre. Pupils could be assessed as groups, their skill at working together becoming a significant element in the mark scheme.

Compared with the proposed GCSE these questions are simple, practicable and inexpensive. They are designed for use by the full ability range, emphasising response rather than different levels of questioning. There is no need for more or less difficult papers and questions (or complicated combinations of both) for able or less able candidates. Pupils can show the quality of their reasoning, whether superficial or profound. Children's responses are the basis for whatever discrimination is required. APU survey tests have shown that similar techniques can be applied in Mathematics, Language and Science; all pupils take the same test papers. All-ability examinations are difficult to devise only if the methodology employed is abstract and literary or if examiners are highly prescriptive about the factual or conceptual knowledge expected of candidates. Open, response-based assessment is, however, insufficiently precise or controlled to press the best students to their limits, exposing weak spots and checking mastery of specific theoretical points. Students themselves are left to decide how far to develop or analyse an idea. This deficiency is relatively unimportant provided examiners are content with 'broad bands' of discrimination and fewer grades. The quality of response to these examples measured on a five-point scale (i.e. A–E or similar) would offer a sufficient basis for an element of selection.

Assessment items designed according to these principles, reflecting a similar movement in classrooms towards cooperative learning and active participation, will contribute to the development of genuinely comprehensive education. In practice these methods should erode the confidence and security of conventional examinations with their continued interest in a self-help lottery.

Question 1

President Kennedy was shown this picture of Cuba in October 1962. Select one of the courses of action open to him from the list below and explain why you think it might be a solution to the crisis.

1. Pre-emptive strike. Fighter bombers to attack the site shown to knock it out. Air chiefs predict 95 per cent success.

2. Blockade Cuba and prohibit entry of warheads and other military equipment. Confrontation would follow if the Russians react unfavourably.

3. Diplomatic pressure through the United Nations for Russian withdrawal.

4. Offer to give up US bases in Turkey in exchange for a Soviet withdrawal from Cuba.

5. Ignore the Cuban threat. Soviet nuclear capability already more than adequate for the destruction of the United States.

Question 2

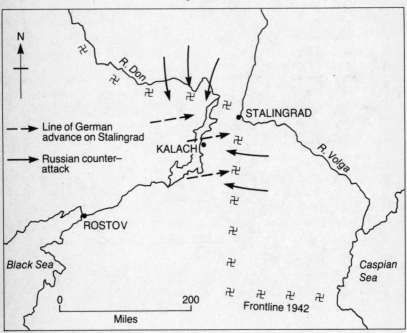

When should the Germans have decided to withdraw during the Battle of Stalingrad? Select one of the dates from the sequence below and give reasons for your choice.

7th September 1942: German Sixth Army offensive with 250,000 men under General von Paulus reaches outskirts of Stalingrad.

End of September: Stalin cables General Zhukov (Russian Deputy Supreme Commander): 'The situation at Stalingrad is getting worse. The enemy is two miles from Stalingrad.

Stalingrad may be taken today or tomorrow if the Northern group of forces does not give immediate help.'

14 October: Paulus weakening flanks (at the rate of one division every five days owing to heavy losses) to send in reserves, but Stalingrad looks as though it will fall.

End October: Weather sharply deteriorating – masses of ice begin to flow down the Volga. Paulus overestimates forces opposing him in Stalingrad street-fighting, so believing that most of the Russian army is tied down in the city

29th October: General Dumitrescu, commanding a much weakened Romanian army on Paulus's left flank, north-west of the city, reports substantial build-up of Russian troops on the east bank of the Don.

11th November: Germans launch final push to take city, committing all reserves. Fought to a standstill by 12th November although Russians have suffered heavy losses.

19th November: Russians counter-attack, sweeping Dumitrescu aside.

20th November: Zeitzler (Head of German General Staff) telephones Hitler: 'Overwhelming Russian forces have broken through the Romanian Third and Fourth Armies north and south of Stalingrad. Their clear intention is to encircle Paulus. Permission, Fuhrer, to withdraw Sixth Army westward to the Don before it is trapped.'

23rd November: Encircling Russians meet, denying the Germans a bridge over the Don and cutting them off from rail communications.

The future

Public and political pressures make it likely that some form of individualised examining and labelling will survive for some years, despite a growing emphasis on shared experience and learning. Common schools should respond positively to this reality, helping devise forms of assessment that have a constructive purpose for most pupils and minimise the damaging consequences of selection and competition. Tests should not be built around pre-set objectives and artificial criteria; the aim should be to design items that reinforce group learning strategies and provide every pupil with a reasonable opportunity to perform confidently on familiar ground.

Teachers should regard assessment as a means of studying the process of learning and of listening attentively to pupils' responses. A question can be thought of as a probe, sensitive to light and sound, able to convert classroom activities into quite definite images. There is no value in items that prompt mistakes or induce candidates to leave blank pages, as if their life's net were empty. Examinations in which many pupils score humiliatingly poor results should be stopped as anti-educational and pointless from every point of view.

Successful learning in the common school will eventually be judged by more appropriate criteria. Learning will come to be seen as a social process in which communities extend their experiences of language and life, rather than as an exercise of memory. Teachers will encourage youngsters to search for an always incomplete understanding, not to create finished products. Achievement will be measured in terms of a group's effectiveness as a team, not the perfection of a single gifted individual. Society will one day recognise that merit is an abundant human quality, not a scarce jewel unfit for streets and factories, nor to be defined in abstractions distant from the people's life. Assessment should foster a self-conscious awareness of strategies in the making, enabling teachers and pupils to measure progress and redirect their efforts as each landmark is reached.

CHAPTER 7

Towards the common school?

It is still possible, despite all expectation, for comprehensive schools to rescue themselves from their present dilemma and recover the initiative in the struggle for a democratic society. Chapters 3 to 6 propose a team-based management structure; a balanced and varied programme of activities as a starting point for group enquiry; and assessment instruments to support learning as it grows from experience. The strategy is to stimulate a new, confident partnership through which teachers can enable young citizens to gain control over their own lives. In future their relationship should be designed to promote 'arrogance' in Aneurin Bevan's sense (see above, p. 8), to encourage a dialogue amongst the pupils themselves animated by curious, critical questioning and leading to fearless, independent maturity. Teachers will not seek or give answers to closed questions but help students to take decisions for themselves, explaining how to apply common sense and how to tolerate uncertainty. An open-minded, enquiring, judicious spirit must be fostered rather than assumed; adults will organise and lead but in relation to knowledge and learning there will be no masters or servants.

The place of the teacher

This prescription differs from others like it by emphasising the role of the teacher as an essential, guiding authority and in rejecting familiar forms of individual rationalism. Pupils are not set off on a trail of independent free enquiry and the aim is not a rootless individual without settled values or convictions making up his own mind about everything. The model for relationships in the classroom is that of the basketball lesson sketched on page 38. Learning here is not democratic in form; the coach is organiser and director. He has a plan, conceived in advance, although flexibly applied. It is disclosed to the pupils a stage at a time, and control is vital to the proceedings. A blow on the whistle and everything stops; if it does not, a rebuke is needed. The process is, however, participatory. Pupils contribute to the learning of themselves and others. Activity is the guiding principle providing an unfolding experience for all those taking part.

Pupils' sense of their own worth and value is promoted; they are encouraged to accept responsibility and develop relationships. Each sub-group has to organise itself. In the classroom the same method would substitute talk for passes and imagination for fitness; the emphasis would be upon cooperative relationships and discussion focused on an experiment or problem. Youngsters can organise ball games themselves (the educational significance of playgrounds deserves closer attention) but what is learned in such circumstances is quite different from and inferior to the coaching session outlined here. As things are, children often contrive to learn a great deal from one another despite their lessons.

The independent judgement and maturity towards which this strategy leads should not be confused with the critical mastery individuals can achieve through private study. Comprehensive learning depends upon relationships between pupils from the same neighbourhood. Knowledge is mediated by social experience and children understand what it means to be human from their involvement in the group. Students are not left to reinvent morality or define themselves outside the framework of tradition; they take part, rather, in the extension of the community through its encounter with the school's teaching. Success is defined to mean the group's progressive understanding of its own political structure and growing ability to manage local affairs. The group uses natural neighbourhood language as a bridge to the powerful dimension of formal discourse and to ensure that no pupil is needlessly excluded.

This argument can be objected to on the grounds that the authority of Headteachers and their colleagues is inimical to the twin objectives of liberty and self-determination. Some believe the initiative must come from the child and that growth and development are inhibited by authority whether benign or repressive. The assumption of these proposals in contrast is that teachers are a yeast whose management and control are a necessary dynamic in generating relationships and ensuring their purposefulness. A good coach, a good editor and a good director set their clients worthwhile tasks, help them establish teams and reinforce the self-confidence of the questioning sensibility. This definition is not an apologia for professional defensiveness or exclusiveness, nor is it another guise for self-centred pedagogy. The intention is to suggest how an experience of learning can be shared, not to reconstruct individual expertise and specialism in the person of the teacher.

There are grounds for such optimism. Extracurricular and public activities already demonstrate teachers' creative ability when their obligations to a system of differentiation and individual success may be forgotten. At an intuitive, impulsive level teachers have now a profound insight into the nature of learning and an unparalleled facility in relations with young people. Some teachers already sense what is needed and their inspired vision permeates sport, drama and music. In its public life the comprehensive school already achieves extraordinary coherence; the habits and methods of the choir, basketball team and drama club need now to invade and colonise the private world of classroom lessons. Teachers should follow their instincts and sympathies rather than the logic of an archaic and discredited system of instruction. All children are in some degree 'bright' or 'intelligent' and need only opportunities to prove their worth. This may be best achieved in an apprenticeship or dialogue with their teachers. Virginia Woolf asked for a similar partnership with the common reader, whom she addressed in these words:

> In your modesty you seem to consider writers are of a different blood and bone from yourselves . . . Never was there a more fatal mistake. It is this division between reader and writer, this humility on your part, these professional airs and graces on ours, that corrupt and emasculate the books which should be the healthy offspring of a close and equal alliance between us.[1]

Children's quiet humility, which many teachers readily accept as evidence that IQ tests are right after all, is the principal obstacle to an equal alliance and it is for this reason that their arrogance must be cultivated.

This emphasis upon personality (in Keatinge's sense, see pp. 34–35) and relationships signifies something other than a desire to improve the quality of individual human beings. It is tautologous and eventually vacuous to argue that education will be improved by 'better' teachers. Schools should not depend upon gifted teachers or seek out bright pupils. Instead the diverse, varying talents of staff and children should be mobilised to advance the common cause. Teaching performance is as indefinable, inexplicable and changing as intelligence. The techniques and group activities described are intended to help teachers as well as taught to work together in teams and discover strategies to increase the quality of school experience. Some will achieve more than others but everyone will be more effective in combination than singly.

Three schools

Teachers will be uncertain of their success and wonder what difference the common school has made. Educational research can provide periscope glimpses of positive changes based on scientific observation but the profession is not easily reassured or convinced. The published APU surveys, for example, have little influence because they report on learning with the people left out, describing the fruits of dialogue but not the faces around the workbench. It is the limitation of objective enquiry. Children's learning is not easily defined or assessed[2] and when attention is shifted from the acquisition of specific skills to the quality of experience in general difficulties multiply.

Fluency of speech, ready wit or a painter's eye are not parcels to be carried from a lesson in a satchel; the understanding of a mature citizen is to be contrasted rather than compared with the skill of an advanced motorist. A student's developing self-possession draws on so many sources that the contribution of particular activities escapes definition. It may be years before events and connections reveal their true value. Adult achievement (especially in the arts) is so distant from its beginnings that it seems magical: the continuous, formless process of learning as invisible as a conjuror's constant practice. Teachers are too remote from their consequences to earn much credit and the frenetic life of the common school is not therefore susceptible to anything more definite than intuitive or provisional judgements.

Fortunately it is easier to recognise successful learning and to discriminate between different educational environments than to measure them on a standard scale. The attitude of pupils and the atmosphere of corridors and classrooms suggest whether or not a school is meeting the needs of all its pupils. A method's effectiveness can be judged from the writing, comments and animation of the children; teachers are accustomed to adapting theory and practice by trial and error.

The contrasting learning experiences created by different teaching strategies can be imaginatively reconstructed by visualising three distinctive dramatic productions, each representing an approach to the problems of education.

Grammar school

A lively director, steeped in the tradition of Shakespeare and the literary culture of university English, sets about the official play. S/he is fastidious in the use of language and uncompromising about 'correct' pronunciation. The text is a 'classic', Thornton Wilder, Oscar Wilde, Bernard Shaw or Shakespeare. Experts are enlisted to ensure high technical standards. A Physics teacher manages the lights; a Needlework mistress and some 'mums' sew the costumes; the Head of Art is set designer, while the Head of Craft is master builder. The Music department contributes a tape to lend

atmosphere as the spring morning is revealed. Discovering
and selecting the school's most talented actors and dramatis
personae requires several auditions; agonising decisions are
taken in casting. Is the voice strong enough? Is he a natural
performer? Is she going to remember the lines? What do those
legs look like in tights? Rehearsals involve some ten or fifteen
of the most socially self-confident and verbally competent
students, with additional deaf-mutes bearing spears or swords
or dressed as domestic servants. On the three nights of the
show the audience comprises a self-selected school intel-
ligentsia, there as theatre-fanciers or to re-enact a distant
memory of youth.[3]

Reorganised school

The Drama department struggles to imitate traditional forms.
If a few good actors are chosen many children who enjoy
Drama will be left out. There is a risk that the specialist Drama
teacher may be an inadequate director but others will be
reluctant to interfere in the area. If a large cast is decided upon
in the hope of greater involvement, management skills of a
new order are required. Rehearsals and production details
need to be meticulously planned to avoid actors waiting in
idleness for their scenes. In the absence of teamwork and
efficient coordination the set is nowhere near ready a few days
before the first night; lines are not learned and the cast seems
ill-chosen. Everyone is disappointed in some way, inwardly
sensing what is unfulfilled or lost. The absence of authority
and definition is almost tangible as systems suitable for one
context fail in another.

Common school

The director values language in all its richness, at ease
with people however they speak and delighting in image and
idiom rather than split infinitives or spellings. S/he enjoys
Shakespeare but his/her own roots are in performance and
drama, in workshop sessions with groups improvising and
expressing their own commentary on life. The production
involves more than one form; not in an experimental sense but
genuinely blending song, dance, music and movement.
Drawing on an expressive, creative tradition concerned pri-

marily with development and communication, the aim is to explore several ideas or levels at once, to escape preoccupation with plot or narrative. As many children as possible are involved, demanding exceptional organisational skills and threatening a high risk of failure. Important parts are performed by students good at Drama but their gifts depend upon and contribute towards the effect of the whole. Specialist teachers similarly offer their expertise but the task is to create and involve teams in the general scheme, helping pupils to do the necessary work on lighting, costumes and set. The audience includes the parents of all those taking part (whether as actors, musicians, dancers or technicians) and a wider community reached through the diverse aspects of the entertainment.

Quality of performance in such drama is not comparable with professional theatre. Shows produced within the community have their own panache, skill, momentum and enjoyment. School drama and sport have an excellence and natural quality that transcends the technically superior activity of professional actors or athletes. The community drama model does not replace literary excellence or attempt to compete with it; there is, rather, a different emphasis and purpose. The theatrical presentation in itself is no longer the sole focus of the product. What is offered in the school version is a process of drawing together performers, presenters, technicians and audience through shared pleasure in shared action. Those who are gifted in some sense (the more various the better) do not diminish or outshine the rest but enhance the experience and contribution of every participant.

Theories of learning and management can transform a whole school, just as the methods applied in this last example enrich experiences of Music or Drama. Teachers help others grow.

The neighbourhood and its critics

While many are reluctant to believe that school can be as enjoyable or purposeful as this, there is a stronger current of scepticism about the possibility that lessons may influence the world outside. The idea that schools might became the focus for their neighbourhoods, aiding the recovery of social cohesion and meaning, has been almost given up. Statistics showing a marked differential in performance between middle- and working-class children are often cited to show that schools are creatures of an economic substructure, not formative agents in their own right. The chasm between rich and poor, the workings of the housing market, the flight from inner cities and racial/ethnic conflict seem evidence of a gulf beyond a teacher's reach.

It has become commonplace to discount the influence of public education. When Michael Rutter's team reported[4] that schools could make a difference to the behaviour of their pupils, the research was received with surprise, an indication of the pervasiveness of class explanations of educational achievement. Many commentators no longer believe that learning can change people's lives and argue that working-class children have a less rich culture and less access to literacy than in the past. Their point is that advertising, television, radio and the popular press are more powerful agents than any curriculum or teacher, and manipulate taste and judgement rather than develop independence.

Richard Hoggart's *Uses of Literacy*, for example, describes the effect of the popular media of the 1950s on what he represents as the authentic working-class community of the industrial North. In his view the culture of working people has lost much of its wholesomeness and texture *since* the advent of mass secondary education, although he does not state the connection explicitly. People are more gullible and less discriminating; their communities less warm and coherent. Hoggart argues that there is a:

> possible interplay between material improvement and cultural loss; that it is probably easier to merge working-class people into a larger, culturally characterless class when they no longer have such strong economic pressure as makes them feel the great importance of loyal membership of their known groups . . . genuine class culture is being eroded in favour of the mass opinion, the mass recreational product and the generalised emotional response. The world of club-singing is being gradually replaced by that of typical radio dance-music and croon-

ing, television cabaret and commercial radio variety . . . The old forms of class culture are in danger of being replaced by a poorer kind of classless . . . 'faceless' culture.[5]

The masses are supposed, therefore, to be enslaved by the language and images of powerful interest groups; Britain is said to be a polarised society with no basis for a common school. There are indeed features of modern society that are not conducive to the emergence of self-governing communities. People's work is separated from their homes, leading to isolation and loneliness on many estates. Mass production has standardised some aspects of life.

On the other hand, there is an underlying coherence and unity created by a shared experience of living. Tens of millions drive their own cars, have telephones, pay mortgages, build extensions or install double glazing and central heating. Broad swathes of the population share in a comfortable existence made possible by electronics and mass production, watching television in houses built by Wates, Wimpey and Barratt to similar designs. Past peculiarities of mining villages, Whitby fishermen, Sheffield iron tradesmen, Preston weavers, Manchester merchants and London lawyers are now secondary to a common thread of private estates and consumer durables. Questions of status and self-esteem, style and self-image are still important in both politics and advertising, but a new language is required.

This society is far from impoverished or uniform. A common lifestyle does not mean that people lose the ability to form groups that are diverse and rich in culture. The vitality of British society can be estimated by reflecting on the kind of life led by the London marathon runners, members of the National Housewives' Register, singers, instrumentalists and actors in thousands of concerts and productions, or those who have made possible the recent phenomenon of the garden centre. Does the factory production of flowers imperil the delight of the herbaceous border? The noticeboard of a town library or Yellow Pages gives a sample of the host of active, lively people who have freedom and enjoyment in their myriad groups. Society cannot be dismissed as monolithic or uniform, passive or in some other sense inferior to what obtained in the past without more detailed evidence.

Richard Hoggart's anxiety about a classless, modern culture, for example, depends on two doubtful hypotheses. The first is that at some previous point working-class life possessed a warmth, solidarity, dignity and decency that arose from a shared experience of chastening poverty. The second is the complaint that consumerism, advertising and newspapers have created a pathetic, passive 'admass' unable to participate in their own lives except as dreamers of other people's dreams. There is something condescending about this line of social criticism. Writers seem to exempt themselves from the contagion they describe; it is people unlike themselves who comprise the 'masses', hapless victims of tele-messages.

There is a strange conservatism about those who reject the new, complex, plural society, preferring instead a version of vanished misery steeped in nostalgia. Can a comparison between events in Salford streets in 1900 and a Wimpey estate today much advance the understanding of contemporary life? The drive towards literacy and creative activity of all kinds seems undiminished by the influence of the media; the negative effect of entrenched class attitudes upon people's willingness to learn seems to be less each year. The cultural achievement of secondary education since 1945 should not be underestimated for the sake of folk memory.

Literacy and education

A continuing growth in literacy seems a more secure historical fact. The English common reader, as ancient as printing, is more common than is often admitted. From the beginning readers and writers shared the almost unlimited potential of the printing press. Bibles in English were the foundation of a verbal imagery that has sustained Christians, Chartists and Socialists, the poor as well as the rich. Working-class radicalism from an early date relied on newspapers like the *Poor Man's Guardian*. Dissenters in politics as in religion used the same language as their orthodox rivals; they were men determined to master printed words as well as those spoken in mill or workshop and to participate in a national debate made possible by these means. Churches, lending libraries, adult evening

classes, colleges, schools, universities and mechanics' insti-
tutes have ensured a broad basis for literacy. The printing press
created a public language for all to share.

Writers have not, on the whole, addressed themselves to
minorities or particular classes. They have written, rather, for
an imaginary English common reader. Dickens and Thack-
eray were in their time as popular as any modern author. The
twentieth century has seen a rapid growth in the numbers
reading and writing for every purpose from art to administration. School leavers are expected to achieve some improvement on their parents' standard of literacy and a major advance
on their grandparents' use of language. Only the development
of a mass audience could sustain the vast circulations of
newspapers, magazines and books.

Kingsley Amis's famous and revealing remark, 'More
means worse' (applied to the new universities), suggests the
frame of mind in which the 'highbrow' passes comment on
mass society and literacy. He feels that if there are a great many
university degrees this must devalue his own, which has
become a totem of superiority, a symbol of expertise and
social worth. There is a deep unease that the privileges of
priests, intellectuals, and the professions may be diluted or
lost. Experts cannot be expected to welcome widespread
knowledge. Solicitors are not anxious to bring about a legal
world in which anyone can convey a property. The prestige of
the specialist is fortified by a natural scepticism about mass-
produced articles, and the fear that old-fashioned values may
be swallowed up by plastic and machines.

An alternative view would stress the expanded circulation
of the quality press, four-channel television and multi-channel
radio, paperback books and polytechnics, the startling increase in the numbers of students at each stage of education
(i.e. 15+, 16+, 17+, 18+, 21+ and adult) and the national
audience for Open University programmes as but a few
examples of a knowledge revolution affecting every level
and dimension of society. The great change from making
and manufacturing to communications and information-
processing depends as much on literate people as on high
technology. Widespread literacy and ultra-rapid communication systems have the effect of drawing together people

from diverse backgrounds. An administrative, bureaucratic infrastructure is made possible by a common set of assumptions about dialogue and discourse. Technically sophisticated but decentralised cities with complex, mobile but very numerous populations depend upon information for their very survival. Education is as central to the self-renewing dynamism of such a society as steam and iron were to Victorian industrialism. The common school can become the hub of a community now dependent on information.

Citizenship

This shared, literate, common culture, incomplete and imperfect though it is, offers a more promising climate for the comprehensive experience than the bleak forecasts of some sociologists. Obscured by the evident tensions and divisions of modern society there is a consensus about what is important only partially distorted by the language of class. Parents believe that school is fundamental for development, sensing that only through education can their children come to terms with new forms of power and knowledge. There is a deep agreement that one child is as valuable as another and that all children have a potential that in the right circumstances could be realised. Young people are credited with possibilities beyond their parents. The hope that these aspirations might be fulfilled through a common curriculum and new teaching methods is too easily discounted in arguments that stress fragmentation and conflict.

In areas like Cambridgeshire and Leicestershire the village college idea has enriched the social and intellectual life of many localities. Schools are the centre of many neighbourhoods and are the part of local government with which people most readily identify. The separatism and divisiveness of the grammar/secondary modern scheme of things has disappeared for most districts, although independent schools and a few surviving authorities persist in detaching 'bright' children from their neighbourhoods. Britain remains an open, muddled society not yet controlled by merit or technology. Schools could become influential in developing a revival in citizenship and self-government. Although the opportunity has not been seized, it has not been entirely lost either.

Through the sustained, active dialogue proposed here teachers and pupils together should aim to extend their understanding of the meaning and techniques of citizenship. There is no need for active involvement or even real understanding if the democratic model adopted is, for example, that of a European election. Citizenship that is little more than a formal gesture, casting one vote into a pool of millions, cannot reasonably become a school's main concern. Attending meetings and casting votes is one, rather symbolic, dimension of citizenship by which cross-flows of instinct and opinion are synthesised into a decision. Elections are a loaded gun pointed at the temples of government, the essential threat behind popular pressure and protest. Real political life is to be found, nevertheless, amongst the tangled social and intellectual threads by which men, women, ideas, knowledge and power are related to one another. Active citizenship should not begin with examination courses in the British Constitution but in a school's determination to influence and change these relationships. The classroom partnership of teachers and pupils can become the dynamic element in a democracy. Shared understanding will lead, perhaps slowly, to shared decisions.

J. Ramsay MacDonald, a neglected political theorist as well as Prime Minister, was among the first to recognise how political and social change might in future flow from people's relationship to new ideas rather than the Labour movement's traditional techniques. MacDonald's emphasis on education rather than industrial or even political action was no mere tactic or excuse for inertia. Indeed, his books constantly warn against change for which the people are unprepared. He believed that the task of Socialists was to 'make enlightenment come quick . . . to coordinate in a movement all the forces that make for organic change'.[6] The power of Socialism for him lay in 'public opinion, not in strikes'. The aim was to create 'by strenuous propaganda the higher and truer conception of a social unity which in a well-ordered society would embrace in harmonious working all those rivalries'. What was needed was 'educational propaganda from the outside, and hard constructive thinking within our own ranks'. Socialism, he said, 'is no class movement. Socialism is a movement of opinion, not an organisation of status. It is not the rule of the working class; it is the organisation of the community.' The self-educated former pupil-teacher did not anticipate the comprehensive school. In the absence of an institutional base he saw politics as a medium through which teachers like himself might educate their communities towards a full understanding of science, industry and social organisation. Like Bevan, however, he saw that education was the only reliable route to a new society.

Since MacDonald's day, powerful techniques have been developed for giving effect to 'opinion'. Television and radio have enlarged the forum for debate, enabling protests to command national attention. Millions believe they are entitled to enter public controversy. Pressure groups like Shelter or Child Poverty Action have taken over some of the functions that once belonged to party politics. Enquiries into nuclear power at Sizewell or a third London airport illustrate the mechanism by which influence is achieved and opinion applied. Individuals who write to the press, or even to the Prime Minister personally, believe that their problem is a fit subject for everyone's concern. MPs, broadcasters, journalists and officials address themselves to an educated mass audience, phrasing their policies with half an ear open for public opinion. Successful politicians study polls rather than speak to or for explicit sectional interests because they have discovered that no class identity has sufficient appeal to sustain a party in power. Political activity is based on the working assumption of an inclusive, open public opinion capable of mature judgement.

In recent years the House of Commons has developed a committee system along United States Congressional lines. Public servants (in local as well as national government) feel themselves to be accountable for their actions and under constant critical scrutiny. The decisions that are not taken reveal as much about democracy as those that are. Issues are considered sensitive and 'political' at remarkably low levels while the debate about access to information suggests how powerful a factor public opinion has become in the calculations of government. Information and communication are as fundamental to this version of democracy as property was for Bagehot's constitution. Once cooperative relationships are firmly established as the natural framework for understanding, decision and action how can schools fail to be of central importance in such a society?

Comprehensive schools have been part of the process by which expectations, opinions and ideas are formed. The quality and inclusiveness of public life in the future depend upon the educational strategies adopted now. Literacy and understanding must be extended so that everyone who chooses to can participate in society. The local, personal contacts and expressions available to all are the basis for helping children towards an articulacy that will develop the range and significance of public opinion. If schools are reformed in the direction suggested in earlier chapters there is every indication that everyone, even the most disadvantaged, can be drawn into an active local community as well as national opinion. No one should underestimate the power of education, least of all those who are themselves educated. If, however, the next generation has little confidence in young people, expressing that pessimism by a renewed emphasis upon the exceptional and the clever, no one should be surprised if those children in their turn lack faith in themselves and run away from Aneurin Bevan's 'fierce light'. The too frequently disparaged social and cultural achievement of the last thirty years has been to open the possibility of citizenship for all despite the vestiges of class and the curse of poverty. Everyone can achieve maturity and judgement through education, but only if teachers remain sufficiently determined and inventive.

Notes and references

Introduction: the idea of a common school

1. See *Aspects of Secondary Education in England: a survey by HM Inspectors of Schools,* HMSO, 1979, especially pp. 82–3 where a remarkable example is recorded: 'An able fourth year group, following an optional course of classical studies, had taken down 100 file pages within a term. A fifth year group in English had written 23,000 words of dictated plot of "Far from the Madding Crowd" . . . Much of this writing was, in one fashion, or another, a re-presentation of teacher or textbook language.'
2. Michael Young, *The Rise of the Meritocracy*, Penguin, 1961 ed., pp. 41–51.
3. Michael Young, op. cit., p. 21.
4. Samuel Smiles, *Self-Help; with illustrations of Character and Conduct*, John Murray, (1859), 1860 ed., pp. 2–5.
5. Quoted in Asa Briggs, *Victorian People*, Penguin, 1965 ed., p. 262. Lowe did not in fact use the more famous phrase 'We must educate our masters.'
6. Robert Owen, *A New View of Society and Report to the County of Lanark*, (1813/21) ed., V. A. C. Gatrell, Penguin, 1969, p. 106.
7. George Orwell, *The Road to Wigan Pier*, Victor Gollancz, 1937, pp. 193–4.
8. Aneurin Bevan, quoted in Michael Foot, *Aneurin Bevan, vol. 1 1897–1945*, MacGibbon and Kee, 1962, fn p. 140 (notes for a meeting of teachers in his constituency).

1 The comprehensive experience today

1. Brian Tyler, Headmaster of Kingswood School, referred to teachers in the private sector during a television interview as 'educational prostitutes'.
2. Peter Dawson, *Making a Comprehensive Work: The Road from Bomb Alley*, Blackwell, 1981.
3. Cf. Michael Rutter *et al.*, *Fifteen Thousand Hours: Secondary Schools and their Effects on Children*, Open Books, 1979.
4. Setting: where pupils are grouped into set 1+ by ability with reference to a single subject. Banding: where pupils are grouped into a band or stream comprising several parallel forms by ability for several subjects. There may be sets within a band.
5. Cf. General Studies Project in 1971.
6. M. W. Keatinge, *Studies in the Teaching of History*, Adam and Charles Black, 1910, pp. 227–8.
7. Op. cit., p. 25.

2 Theories of learning

1. See his *Contrary Imaginations: Psychological Study of the English Schoolboy*, Penguin, 1968.
2. Michael Young anticipated even this development: 'The people who campaigned for the common school constantly attacked the segregation of clever from stupid which it was the purpose of intelligence tests to accomplish' (M. Young, op. cit., pp. 70–74).
3. Assessment issues are examined in Chapter 6.
4. The usefulness of terms like 'imagination' and 'creativity' for curriculum design is discussed on p. 87.
5. See p. 89 for a further discussion.
6. Jean Jacques Rousseau, in *Émile, ou de l'Éducation*, ed. F. and P. Richard (Paris, 1964), advised tutors to abandon beating and rote-learning in favour of practical activity. He followed the development of a typical pupil, Émile. 'Darren' explores the school experience of a modern Émile. Rousseau felt that learning in a woman was 'unpleasing and unnecessary' but what follows here would need little adaptation to apply with equal truth to 'Tracey'.
7. E. M. Forster, *Howards End*, Penguin, 1946 (first published 1910).
8. See, for example, Penelope Leach, *Babyhood: infant development from birth to two years*, Penguin, 1975.
9. and 10. Discussed more fully in Chapter 5.
11. In 'Language and Thought', *Knowledge and the Curriculum*, Routledge, 1974, pp. 69–83.

3 Leadership and change

1. By national agreement schools are allocated posts of responsibility in proportion to the number and age of their pupils.
2. The Stantonbury Campus at Milton Keynes, and Bretton Woods Community School in Peterborough are good examples.
3. Based upon my reading of job descriptions for advertised posts, school handbooks and observation of management structures.
4. Depicted by lines of asterisks (*) in the diagram.
5. See those of Hertfordshire or Cambridgeshire, for example.
6. Education officers, governors, parents, staff and children.
7. Even that is difficult when governors meet only termly.
8. Cf. the Heinemann Organisation in Schools series edited by Michael Marland.
9. See, for example, the series 'Management in Schools' published by Education for Industrial Society, 1982, 1983.
10. T. Taylor, *New Partnership for our Schools*, HMSO, 1977.
11. The proposal implicit here is that the school's senior teacher appointments should be used to extend the management team. A group of five or six teachers (depending on the size of the school and the authority's discretion under Burnham) with a 'whole school' brief is necessary to cover the range of tasks generated by a modern comprehensive school. Senior teacher posts in many schools are used to enhance the prestige of specific, individual assignments (e.g. Head of Sixth Form, Head of Middle School). This is likely to reinforce the idea of solitary teachers tackling 'jobs' and to increase the 'middle management' ambiguity represented in diagram 1.

4 The sceptred curriculum

1. Cf. *A Framework for the School Curriculum*, DES, 1980, or *Curriculum 11–16*, HMSO, 1977.
2. H. Mary Warnock, *Special Educational Needs*, HMSO, 1978.
3. Op. cit.
4. The areas suggested by *Curriculum 11–16*, op. cit., p. 6, are: aesthetic and creative, ethical, linguistic, mathematical, physical, scientific, social and political, spiritual.
5. See pp. 44–45.
6. J. B. Coltham and J. Fines, *Educational Objectives for the Study of History, A Suggested Framework*, Historical Association, Teaching History Series No. 35, 1971.
7. A. Gard and P. J. Lee, 'Educational Objectives for the Study of History Reconsidered' in Dickinson and Lee, *History Teaching and Historical Understanding*, Heinemann, 1978.
8. Ibid., p. 36.
9. Ibid., p. 32.

10. E.g. pressure from teacher unions on the consultative committee.
11. See p. 42 above and following.
12. H. G. Wells, *The New Machiavelli*, Penguin, 1978, p. 26 (first published 1911).
13. See *Aspects of Secondary Education*, op. cit.
14. See pp. 49–53 above.
15. David Holbrook, *English For Maturity*, Cambridge University Press, 1967.
16. Barry Hines, *Kestrel for a Knave*, English Library, 1969.
17. John Gretton and Mark Jackson, *William Tyndale: Death of a School or System*, Allen & Unwin, 1976.
18. See *Black Paper 1975: The Fight for Education*, ed. C. B. Cox and Rhodes Boyson, Dent, 1975. A series of such papers attacking progressive ideas and aspects of comprehensive education succeeded in changing the terms of debate.
19. A. Bullock, *Language for Life*, HMSO, 1975.
20. Ibid., Chapter 6.27.
21. Michael Marland, *Language Across the Curriculum*, Heinemann, 1977.
22. Donald Gould, 'The Springs of Suffering', *New Statesman*, 28 October, 1977.

5 Teaching methods

1. David Hargreaves, *The Challenge for the Comprehensive School*, Routledge, 1982, p. 163.
2. From a note circulated to professional associations by the DES entitled *The Organisation and Content of the 5–16 Curriculum*, 1984.
3. See p. 38 above.
4. See p. 33 and following.
5. Cf. discussion on p. 99.

6 Assessment and examinations

1. Imitating the model of Scouting awards and Associated Board instrumental examinations.
2. Professor D. Nuttall, *The Rasch Model*, internal paper for the Assessment of Performance Unit.
3. Questions 1 and 2, pp. 133–135.

7 Towards the common school?

1. Quoted in Lyndall Gordon, *A Writer's Life*, Oxford, 1984, p. 182.
2. See Chapter 6 on assessment.

3. This production deserves respect. A considerable number of people are brought together to work intensely and cooperatively in a shared and enjoyable enterprise. It is a well-managed show. An 'official' play, well led, can be moving, inspiring and richly rewarding. The problem is reproducing these methods in an inappropriate context.

4. Michael Rutter *et al.*, op. cit.

5. Richard Hoggart, *Uses of Literacy*, Penguin 1960 ed., p. 285.

6. Quoted in and discussed, *Ramsay MacDonald's Political Writings*, ed. Bernard Barker, Allen Lane 1972, pp. 47–8.

Index